MONTH TO- MONTH GARDENING

Tips for

Designing, Growing,

and Maintaining Your

New Mexico Garden

Kelli Dolecek

FOUR SISTERS PUBLISHING, INC.

MONTH-TO-MONTH GARDENING, NEW MEXICO
Copyright © 1999 Four Sisters Publishing, Inc. All rights reserved.
No part of this book may be used or reproduced in any manner whatsoever, or
stored in a database or retrieval system, without prior written permission
from the publisher.

FIRST EDITION

Photography: Roger Speyer, Paul Bousquet
Design: Abbie Kozik Design
Landscape Designs and General Information: Carole Kastler, Camelot Design
Mountain Information, Mountain Landscape Design: Donna Elliott, Elliott & Associates, Inc.
Whimsical Garden Information & Design: Wendy Booth, Ivy Street Design
Interior Garden Illustration: Fresh Ink, Lizabeth Netzel
Design and Desktop: DT Production
Production Coordination and Editing: Elizabeth Gold
Editing: Blue Skies Ahead
Editing: Catherine Dold

ISBN 0-9663566-2-4

Printed in the United States of America.

10 9 8 7 6 5 4 3 2 1

Four Sisters Publishing, Inc.
P.O. Box 3083
Englewood, CO 80155
303-699-2365 (phone)
303-680-6112 (fax)
tdc@usa.net (email)

1-888-Garden-8 (to order)
www.mtmgardening.com

Library of Congress Catalog Card Number: 99-61294

INTRODUCTION

There is no absolute right or wrong in how things are done to achieve success in gardening. The best testament to what works and what doesn't is experience. And that's what **MONTH–TO–MONTH GARDENING, NEW MEXICO** brings you — nearly 100 years of New Mexico gardening expertise.

The gardening and maintenance experts in this book have seen thousands of New Mexico gardens and talked with thousands of their owners. Their ideas are based on real-life experience, not theoretical know-how. If anyone can tell you what to do with your New Mexico trees, flowers, shrubs, lawn, vegetables, roses, rocks, interior plants... it's these people!

MONTH–TO–MONTH GARDENING, NEW MEXICO will help you in two ways. One: It quickly covers the essentials you need to know to design, grow, and maintain a New Mexico garden. It's geared to people who don't have time to do extensive research, read long, complicated books, or learn totally by trial and error. Two: The when in New Mexico is just as important as the how. The book is divided into 12 months that give you over 250 of the best ideas for when to grow and when to maintain your garden.

Guarantees? No. But the book offers 12 practical, simple designs for New Mexico landscaping and it equips you with the best and worst plant lists for the state. You will find a New Mexico lawn calendar, a special section on trees and shrubs, and over 90 detailed tips on New Mexico soil, staking, pruning, mulching, insects, weeds, watering, and more. As an extra plus, look for information on which plants bloom when in New Mexico so you can plan on year-round color and contrast in your landscape.

MONTH–TO–MONTH GARDENING, NEW MEXICO is for every person who wants a quick path to feeling comfortable about gardening in New Mexico.

Thanks to Andrew Lisignoli, horticulturist and MONTH–TO–MONTH GARDENING, NEW MEXICO gardening editor, for his excellent efforts in digging deep to find the best gardening information available.

Kelli A. Dolecek

Kelli A. Dolecek

LANDSCAPE AND GARDEN EXPERTS

GARDENING EDITOR,
MONTH–TO–MONTH GARDENING,
NEW MEXICO
Andrew Lisignoli,
Consultant/Horticulturist
Andrew has 27 years experience in horticulture, design, consultation, sales, and service to the landscape and garden center industry, 20 of these spent in New Mexico.

ADDITIONAL EXPERTS
Nancy Stokes, Horticulturist
Nancy has been involved in the nursery industries for 35+ years, 17 of those spent in the New Mexico nursery business.

Paynes Nurseries
304 Camino Alire
Santa Fe, NM 87501
505-988-8011
nursery@rt66.com

James R. Sais, Horticulturist
Jim retired after 33 years as a full professor and Northern District Department Head for the New Mexico Cooperative Extension Service. He has also written a weekly garden column for the Albuquerque Journal *and currently has a call–in gardening program on KKOB Radio. Jim is a native New Mexican!*

Rowland Nursery, Inc. and
All Seasons EnviroScapes
7402 Menaul, N.E.
Albuquerque, NM 87110
505-883-5727

Willie Kutac
Willie worked for the government for 25 years as an agronomist specializing in soils and soil chemistry. He has owned and managed Kutips Nursery since 1972.

Kutips Nursery
1817 Schofield Lane
Farmington, NM 87401
505-325-6602

GARDENING EDITOR,
MONTH–TO–MONTH GARDENING
Ruth Stadler, Horticulturist
303-730-1920
rstadler@pcisys.net

TABLE OF CONTENTS

NEW MEXICO GARDENING CAN BE TOUGH...

People who like to dig in the soil — and water and mix and prune and plant and weed and plan — do so for many reasons. But everyone who attempts to landscape and garden has one basic need in common: to get results.

Do you know of anyone (except kids, maybe) who plays in the dirt just for fun? How about watering weeds — now that's a real good way to get rid of stress. Do you know of anyone who spends hundreds of dollars on plants, seeds, trees, and grass with the expectation that they will all die? The bottom line in landscaping and gardening is simple: You have to get results that you can see, feel, touch, and smell.

In New Mexico, you have to work at your gardening a little harder than in other parts of the country. Many would call it just plain impossible, but most people learn to accommodate themselves to the "New Mexico Negatives," and end up with beautiful landscapes and gardens for their efforts.

Three New Mexico Negatives make landscaping and gardening tough:

New Mexico soil isn't the best. And just to make it really tough, there are several kinds of poor soil in New Mexico: rocky soil, sand, and clay. Some areas have all three, others have clay, and the people next door may have sand. There are numerous places that have layers of caliche (soil that is cemented by particles of calcium or magnesium). Amending the soil in New Mexico is the solution for this Negative. While it does take some time, there are many rewards that come from modifying the soil nature gave to New Mexico.

New Mexico is dry and windy. New Mexico, as a general rule, does not get a lot of moisture. (It varies from an average of 7" per year in the South and South Central areas to 14" in the North and North Central areas of the state.) In addition, there are parts of the state that get a lot of wind. On top of both of these drying factors, the sun is very intense. Little water, wind, and lots of harsh sun are not a healthy combination for flowers, trees, shrubs, and grasses. What, where, when, and how to plant are the solutions for this Negative.

New Mexico has extreme temperature fluctuations. Some days, the temperature rises to 60°, only to drop into the high teens at night. During some weeks, you will see rain, sleet, snow, and, of course, sunshine (the sun shines about 300 days of the year). This ongoing fluctuation of temperature is hard on not only plants, but on other elements in your landscape including patios, artwork, and water features as well. The solution for this Negative is to select the best plants and protect them, so the temperature fluctuations won't affect them as much.

New Mexico also boasts many garden blessings. Lack of moisture (and, therefore, low humidity) means we have relatively few problems with insects and diseases. All those days of sunshine bring vibrant, bright flowers. For some, a shorter growing season is a blessing, leaving time for other activities.

So, if you like to dig in the soil — and water and mix and prune and plant and weed and plan — and you happen to live in New Mexico... you can still get results. Your success will fill your senses after you're done.

A note on how to use MONTH-TO-MONTH GARDENING, NEW MEXICO:

Many plant labels, garden centers, and catalogs refer to "zones." U. S. Department of Agriculture plant hardiness zones are a guide (based on average winter minimum temperatures) to tell you what plants will live in your particular area. They also give you a good idea of when it's safe to plant to avoid frost damage.

There are three primary zones in New Mexico: Zone 5 in the North and North Central areas, including Santa Fe; Zone 6 in the East, parts of the West, and South Central areas, including Albuquerque; and Zone 7 in the South, including Las Cruces. Conservatively, Zone 5 areas have a growing season of approximately 105 days; Zone 6 has a growing season of approximately 130 days; while the growing season in Zone 7 is approximately 175 days. You're safe from frost after May 31 in Zone 5, after about May 17 in Zone 6, and as early as April 27 in Zone 7.

If you are unsure about what the gardening zone is where you live, check with a garden center near you.

Throughout the book, we use the term "higher elevations" to define those areas in New Mexico that are above 5,000 feet. Generally, if you live in the higher elevations, you will want to complete the spring maintenance tips one month later and the fall maintenance tips one month earlier than those people who live in the high desert South and South Central areas of the state. There are some more arid Zone 8 pockets, particularly in the South. Spring garden maintenance in these areas would take place about one month earlier than the rest of New Mexico.

PERENNIALS/ ANNUALS/ BULBS

✳ Check stored bulbs to make sure they haven't sprouted or rotted. (See page 59.)

✳ Place orders for seeds and other mail-order plants or check with your local garden center.

✳ Plant pansies in lower elevations.

✳ Sow seeds indoors for petunias, marigolds, asters, and dianthus. (See page 8.) (You also can buy transplants at garden centers in April.)

✳ Test saved seeds from last season to see if they'll sprout.

Want to test seeds saved from the last gardening season? Here are some ideas:

Place about ten seeds between sheets of a damp paper towel and then seal the paper towels in a plastic food storage bag.

Keep the paper towel damp and the bag out of direct sun.

Check daily to see if the seeds have sprouted. If less than half sprout, toss the bunch.

Plant those that have sprouted in containers indoors for setting out in April or May!

FEBRUARY
MAINTENANCE TIPS

....

....

....

....

....

....

....

There are several basic rules to follow when ordering seeds or plants via mail. Make sure what you are ordering can live in your area. Ask if there will be substitutions made if a plant is out-of-stock and let them know if substitutions are acceptable. Confirm that plants were propagated in a nursery (ask where) and not dug up from some rural area of the country. Date seed packages when they arrive and keep a copy of your order form. If you want to be very sure about what you are getting, shop at your local garden center.

FEBRUARY
MAINTENANCE TIPS

....

....

....

....

....

....

....

Ornamental grasses are flexible, year–round plants for the New Mexico landscape. They can be interspersed with evergreen shrubs and trees for the winter garden, they can be planted for erosion control on steep slopes, their unique shapes and colors are appealing when mixed with perennials and annuals in the garden, and stems can be cut for indoor flower arrangements. A variety of ornamental grasses will grow in New Mexico; some of the most popular include blue fescue, blue avena, feather reed, pampas, maiden grasses, sand love, Japanese blood grass, fountain, and feather grass.

TREES AND SHRUBS

❋ Plant container and balled and burlapped trees and shrubs late this month in lower elevations. (See How-To Tip on page 120.)

❋ Gently brush the snow off trees and shrubs in higher elevations.

❋ In higher elevations, prune away any branches that have been injured or torn because of ice, wind, and snow.

❋ In lower elevations, prune fruit trees.

❋ Apply dormant oil.

❋ Thin old, overgrown deciduous shrubs (see page 9), before they start to bud out or bloom. (See How-To Tip on page 119.)

ROSES

❋ Make decisions on which roses to replace; choose where you want to transplant or plant new roses.

LAWN

❋ Check Lawn Maintenance Calendar. (See page 150.)

❋ Rake and aerate the lawn in lower elevations. (See page 22.)

* Fertilize the lawn in lower elevations. (See How-To Tip on page 114.) (Be sure to check your irrigation system *before* you fertilize and aerate.)

* In lower elevations, apply a pre-emergent herbicide to your lawn if you've had crabgrass problems in the past. Do before mid-March when the crabgrass germinates. (See page 16.)

* Sharpen the blades and tune up your lawn mower in lower elevations.

KITCHEN GARDEN

* Sow seeds indoors toward the end of the month for peppers, eggplant, broccoli, cabbage, and tomatoes.

* In lower elevations plant garlic, onions, potatoes, and peas.

* Plan your kitchen garden for planting using garden center transplants available March to mid-May. (See page 23.)

Need a few tips on what to plant in your kitchen garden? Here are some ideas:

Check that the plants you want to grow will be ready for harvesting before the end of your growing season. Each vegetable and herb needs a specific soil temperature before it will germinate and grow.

FEBRUARY
MAINTENANCE TIPS

When starting plants from seeds indoors, use only clean, new, plastic pots and virgin potting soil. Plant the seeds at a depth of three times their width unless the seed is very small, then plant it nearer to the surface. Keep the soil damp at all times, but not wet. The soil cannot dry out. Mist the seedlings as they start to grow. Some seeds need light to germinate.

FEBRUARY
MAINTENANCE TIPS

If you live in higher elevations, you can extend the growing season beyond 105 days using greenhouses, cold frames, or plant protectors.

INTERIOR GARDEN

❋ Thoroughly clean all indoor plants. (See How-To Tip on page 111.)

❋ Wash or replace all plant saucers to get rid of salt build-up.

GENERAL

❋ Prune fruit-bearing vines back on a day when the temperature is above 32°. Pruning promotes bushy vines in the spring, which means more fruit. (Grapes in lower elevations should be pruned back in late March.)

Need help on pruning vines? Here are some ideas:

The best time to prune vines is now, when they are still dormant. If you can't do it now, wait until after they have bloomed before pruning.

It's good gardening practice to thin out old, overgrown shrubs in New Mexico in late winter. This encourages the shrub to grow from the base of the plant, rather than on the existing branches, which makes for a better looking and healthier shrub. If you prune in the winter, you will have little or no shearing work (not recommended on shrubs, anyway) in the spring. Prune butterfly bushes, blue mist spirea, and chamisa hard (12" from the ground) to encourage fresh new growth and more blooms.

Do not prune vines that have vertical suckers until summer if you want to dwarf or stunt their growth to keep them from invading trees, shrubs, and flower beds.

Prune vines back by as much as half their length.

FEBRUARY
MAINTENANCE TIPS

✳ Do not add ashes from fireplaces or wood burning stoves to the soil around your plants. The ash can create a salt imbalance.

✳ Buy or order garden tools.

✳ Prepare the soil for lower elevation gardens. (See How-To Tip on page 127.)

✳ Deep water trees, shrubs and roses as needed. (See How-To Tip on page 113.)

✳ Leave the compost pile alone.

The truth about aspens: They are happiest at 6,500 feet or above. If you plant them lower than this, they will require more care. Be particular about how you water them, expect problems with inkspot and leafspot diseases (more a cosmetic issue than life–threatening), oyster shell scale (must deal with or the tree could die), and aphids. You can expect a short life span with aspens – plus or minus 20 years – but they sucker, so this keeps them coming back without having to purchase more. Overall, while difficult to keep healthy, aspens can be a valuable asset to the landscape.

SPRING

March, April, May

MARCH
MAINTENANCE TIPS

....

....

....

....

....

....

....

Annuals: These plants, whether grown from seed or in the form of transplants, will only live for one growing season. Then they set seed and die. Annuals are known for their vivid, bright colors. Perennials: Perennials are the plants that come back every year. They often provide the "substance" in the garden, because you know you can count on them to grow each year in the same place as the last year. Bulbs: There are true bulbs, as in tulips and daffodils, then there are also rhizomes, tubers, corms, and tuberous roots, as in iris, ranunculas, and crocus. We use the common gardening term "bulb" to describe all of these throughout the book.

PERENNIALS/ ANNUALS/ BULBS

✻ After removing dead blooms, fertilize bulb plants that were planted in the fall with a complete fertilizer.

✻ Plant perennial transplants and pansies.

✻ If plants are starting to bud out, gradually push back extra mulch (over the next month) that protected plants through the winter.

✻ Check stored bulbs (cannas, dahlias, gladiolus) for sprouting.

✻ Young plants may suffer when first put in the ground because of New Mexico's high sun intensity, temperature fluctuations, and wind. Protect them with a "row cover" available at garden centers and nurseries or spray them with liquid seaweed or liquid potassium.

✻ If you haven't already done so, cut back perennials (except evergreen perennials — plants that stay green all year) from last year. With a sharp pair of pruning shears or scissors, remove dead plant material all the way to the ground. (Wait until April for higher elevations.) (See page 62.)

* You can divide perennial plants at this time. (Wait until April for higher elevations.) (See page 19.)

* Put out seed for hardy annuals such as bachelor's button, calendula, larkspur, pansy, and snapdragon. (Wait until April for higher elevations.)

TREES AND SHRUBS

* Check evergreens for browning and deciduous trees and shrubs for branches and buds that have died. Take out the dead wood on deciduous trees and shrubs and prune the brown branches from evergreens. (See How-To Tip on page 119.)

* Fertilize evergreens and deciduous trees and shrubs. (See How-To Tip on page 114.) (Wait until late April in higher elevations.)

* Fertilize (with iron and other trace minerals) maples, wisteria, roses or other plants that tend to get yellow in the middle of the summer.

* If you didn't rake leaves or remove old fruit from fruit and deciduous trees in the fall, do so now.

* Spray pine tree trunks for pinon scale. (Wait until early May in higher elevations.)

MARCH
MAINTENANCE TIPS

While leaves from healthy trees can provide a mulch, those from diseased trees can spread the disease back to the tree and other surrounding plants the next growing season. Control insects like aphids, mites, and scale by raking up dead leaves from the previous season.

MARCH
MAINTENANCE TIPS

❋ Prune junipers. (See How-To Tip on page 119.)

❋ Plant container and balled and burlapped trees and shrubs late this month. (See How-To Tip on page 120.)

❋ Plant and transplant bare-root trees and shrubs. (See How-To Tip on page 120.) (Wait until April in higher elevations.)

ROSES

❋ Purchase rose bushes in containers for planting. (See How-To Tip on page 118.)

❋ Plant bare-root roses, or transplant existing roses now or as soon as the ground is workable. (See How-To Tip on page 118.)

❋ Prune back rose bushes and remove any remaining winter mulch. (Wait until late April in higher elevations.)

LAWN

❋ Check Lawn Maintenance Calendar. (See page 150.)

❋ If you have an irrigation system, start it up and test it for problems that may have occurred over the winter. Do this before you aerate and before you fertilize!

You can buy rose bushes either in containers or bare-root (usually in bags). Plant bare-root roses before leaves appear on the plant (can be done now or early in April); plant container roses after the last freeze (mid- to late April). Bare-root plants should have several thick canes that are not wrinkled; container bushes should have three or four healthy canes that are green or red and not shriveled up. Check for insects and disease (see How-To Tip on page 129) both on top of and underneath the leaves. Purchase rose bushes that have average to good disease resistance. Store plants in a cool (not freezing) location until planting. Container bushes should be watered periodically so the soil stays damp.

* Water and aerate bluegrass and tall fescue lawns. (See page 22.) Do this before you apply pre-emergent! (Wait until April in higher elevations.)

* Fertilize the lawn. (See How-To Tip on page 114.) (Wait until April in higher elevations.) After fertilizing, sweep off your sidewalks and driveway because the fertilizer containing iron can cause spots that look like rust after watering.

* In higher elevations, apply a pre-emergent herbicide to your lawn before April if you've had crabgrass problems.

Have problems with crabgrass or other weeds? Here are some ideas:

Don't scalp your lawn when mowing. Mow higher.

Don't water lightly and frequently. Water more heavily and less often.

Aerate and fertilize – thick, healthy lawns are less prone to crabgrass.

Fill in any blank spots in the lawn so crabgrass can't invade.

KITCHEN GARDEN

* Sow seeds of peas, onions, carrots, lettuce, spinach, and radishes outdoors. Plant transplants (i.e., seedlings) of broccoli, cabbage, and kale.

MARCH
MAINTENANCE TIPS

You can buy strawberries that are either June–bearing (a big crop once a year), or ever–bearing (the crop produces throughout the summer). Two varieties recommended for New Mexico are Ogalala and Fort Laramie. Strawberries come in containers, bare–root, and sometimes in transplants. Plant strawberries 18" apart in well prepared garden soil (see How–To Tip on page 127), placing the base of the plant at soil level. Plants will produce more berries if they are exposed to more sunlight. To protect strawberries through the winter, mulch with 4" to 6" of straw. If you want a bigger crop, transplant the new plant that has grown at the end of each runner.

MARCH
MAINTENANCE TIPS

* Plant strawberries. (See page 16.)

INTERIOR PLANTS

* Fertilize pots of annuals that were over-wintered indoors.

* Repot root-bound houseplants.

* In higher elevations, plant vegetables and bedding plants in the greenhouse or a sunny window for planting outside in the beginning of June.

GENERAL

* Prepare the soil for all New Mexico gardens except those at higher elevations, where you may need to wait until the ground is workable (usually April or May). In the more arid south, the ground is usually workable in February. (See How-To Tip on page 127.)

* In lower elevations, prune grape vines back on a day when the temperature is above 32°. Pruning promotes bushy vines in the spring, which means more fruit.

* Fork 2" to 3" of well-aged compost into garden beds. This will aerate the root area of plants. (Wait until April for higher elevations.)

If the roots of houseplants are coming out the hole in the bottom of the pot, or if they are wound tightly around inside the pot, you need to repot them. You also can tell if a plant needs repotting because it grows very slowly or dries out quickly after being watered. Clay or plastic pots? Use plastic because they hold the moisture better but do not absorb the salt from the soil. (Watering will draw the salt back out of the clay pot and eventually saturate the plant, which leads to salt poisoning and death.) Use a pot only slightly larger than the last one because many plants thrive when root bound.

PERENNIALS/ ANNUALS/ BULBS

✳ If you haven't already done so, cut back perennials (except evergreen perennials — plants that stay green all year) from last year. With a sharp pair of pruning shears, remove dead plant material all the way to the ground.

✳ Plant and transplant perennials on a cloudy day or in the early evening. Plant at the level of the base of the stem in well-prepared soil. (Perennials can also be planted in the mountains, if the soil is workable. Transplants, not seeds, are recommended.)

Need advice on where to plant perennials? Here are some ideas:

Find out if your plant grows better in the sun or in the shade and plant accordingly. Perennials that like the sun need about six hours of sun a day, and those that like shade should get no more than five hours of morning sun a day.

Remember, perennials come back every year, so find out about how large your plant will get and space accordingly. (Lots of perennials planted close together look beautiful and are easier to weed!

APRIL
MAINTENANCE TIPS

Plant summer flowering bulbs such as allium, dahlias, lilies, cannas, and gladiolus. (Wait until May in higher elevations.) Plant gladiolus in shifts, every few weeks, so they bloom all summer. Make sure the soil is well-prepared (see How–To Tip on page 127) and plant the bulb in a hole that is the same width as the bulb and three times its height. Since the growth will come out of the tip, plant with the tip facing up. Certain types of bulbs don't have a tip and they can be planted in any position. (If in doubt, plant sideways.) Water as needed. You can add bone meal or super–phosphate to the bottom of the hole.

APRIL
MAINTENANCE TIPS

....

....

....

....

....

....

....

The way to divide perennial plants is to dig them up in small clusters (make sure to get the roots). Thrust two gardening forks down the middle of the cluster, dividing it in two. If the cluster is very large, keep the outside growth for replanting and get rid of the inside of the plant because it is the oldest. After planting, water as needed. (See How–To Tip on page 124.) Perennials should be divided every three to four years.

Keep track of what looks good and what doesn't. You can transplant in the fall.

Soak bare–root plants in a bucket of water for about 30 minutes before planting.

✳ In higher elevations, plant seed for hardy annuals and perennials such as snapdragons, bachelor's button, larkspur, California poppy, baby's breath, and pansies.

✳ Take note of when the last killing frost date is for your area and be careful not to plant annuals before this time. (See page 5.)

✳ In higher elevations, fork 2" to 3" of well-aged compost into garden beds. This will not only amend the soil but also aerate the root area of plants.

✳ Divide fall-blooming perennial plants and bulbs in higher elevations.

✳ Plant summer-flowering bulbs.

✳ Seed or overseed wildflower beds if this wasn't done last fall. (See page 56.)

✳ Look for garden center advertisements on flower and vegetable plants.

✳ Cut back ornamental grasses at the base of the plant. (See page 24.)

✻ Plant ground covers.

Ground covers are plants that usually grow low to the ground and spread out. Here are a few things to note:

Ground covers are a good substitute for lawn, although they're not meant for a lot of traffic. Once established, ground covers require little maintenance.

Find out if your ground cover grows better in the sun or in the shade and plant accordingly.

Ground covers should be planted close enough that they will fill in fairly quickly, but not so close that they become over-crowded. The usual standard is to plant them 8" on center (center of plant to center of plant).

Get rid of all weeds before you plant.

✻ Mow (at highest setting) established ground covers to clean them up and remove winterburn.

TREES AND SHRUBS

✻ Thin out old, overgrown shrubs by pruning out no more than one-third of the oldest canes from the base of the shrub. Wait to prune shrubs that are starting to bud out until after they bloom. (See How-To Tip on page 119.)

Be cautious when planting in higher elevations this month! If the winter has been somewhat mild, the soil will be workable, so trees and shrubs can be planted. Plants brought from lower elevations still should be in their dormant state or have minimal leaf expansion since low night temperatures could frost them.

APRIL
MAINTENANCE TIPS

....

....

....

....

....

....

....

Cool season grasses, such as bluegrass, rye, and fescues, perform best during cool (not cold) months of the spring and fall. Warm season grasses, such as buffalo–grass, Bermuda, and blue gramma, grow best during the warmer months of the year. You need to water cool season grasses less in the spring and fall and more in the hot summer months so they'll stay green. While it takes longer for the warm season grasses to turn green, they require much less water than the cool season grasses to stay green during the hottest months of the year. Rake the area smooth and either sod or seed. If you sod, be sure to amend the soil first.

✲ If you used tree wrap, remove it now.

✲ Plant and transplant bare-root, container, and balled and burlapped trees and shrubs. (See How-To Tip on page 120.)

✲ Continue to deep water trees and shrubs. (See How-To Tip on page 113.)

✲ In higher elevations, push back extra mulches around perennials and shrubs.

ROSES

✲ You can still transplant or plant bare-root rose bushes in early to mid-April, as soon as the ground is workable. (See How-To Tip on page 118.)

✲ Gradually remove the mound of mulch from rose bushes.

LAWN

✲ Check the Lawn Maintenance Calendar. (See page 150.)

✲ Aerate the lawn in higher elevations.

✲ Fertilize the lawn in higher elevations. (See How-To Tip on page 114.)

✻ Mow lawn to no less than 2" and never cut any more than one-third of the growth in a single cutting. (In higher elevations lawn probably won't need mowing until early May.)

✻ Seed or sod cool season grasses like bluegrass, rye, and fescues. At lower elevations, apply chemicals for grub control.

KITCHEN GARDEN

✻ Continue watering "cool season" vegetables sowed in February and March.

✻ Hoe or hand-pull spring weeds in the vegetable garden (like dandelions).

GENERAL

✻ Prepare the soil for all New Mexico gardens, if the soil is workable. (See How-To Tip on page 127.)

✻ Look for pest alerts for the pine tip moth. (See How-To Tip on page 129.)

✻ Begin to control weeds at higher elevations. (See How-To Tip on page 123.)

✻ Deep water trees, shrubs, and roses as needed. (See How-To Tip on page 113.)

✻ Turn the compost pile. (See How-To Tip on page 111.)

APRIL
MAINTENANCE TIPS

To aerate the lawn, rent an aerator that will remove plugs of lawn and soil. This will encourage grass roots to grow deeper, which is crucial in New Mexico since we do not have an overabundance of water. Do not spike the lawn because it compacts the soil around where the spike went in.

MAY
MAINTENANCE TIPS

....

....

....

....

....

....

....

When you buy plants for your garden (flower or vegetable), look for six packs of seedlings that are not dried out or soaking wet, not wilted looking or yellow, and not spindly. The plant should be one-third soil depth to no more than two-thirds plant foliage. Look for plants with lots of buds and a few flowers (to give you an idea of color). Look for plants with healthy, compact foliage.

PERENNIALS/ ANNUALS/ BULBS

❋ Mulch around flowers and in shrub beds to conserve moisture and keep down weeds. (See How-To Tip on page 115.)

❋ Plant annual transplants at the same depth as in the container (or slightly higher in very clay soil) in soil-amended beds. (See How-To Tip on page 127.)

❋ Sow annual flower seeds, such as cosmos and zinnias, into the garden. (Be patient, planting from seed will take longer than buying and planting transplants.)

❋ Set out any seedlings sowed indoors.

❋ Check plants for aphids and treat if necessary. (See How-To Tip on page 129.)

❋ Pinch mums so they are bushy in the fall. (See How-To Tip on page 112.)

* Put out annuals and perennials that have been overwintered indoors in pots.

* Plant containers and window boxes with herbs and annuals. Use good potting soil, and water every other day (every day during the summer).

* Rake 2" to 3" of compost into all garden areas and beds in higher elevations.

* Plant ornamental grasses.

TREES AND SHRUBS

* If you shear your hedges, never take off more than one-third of the growth. The top should be more narrow than the base so the sun reaches all areas.

* Spray pine trees, like pinon and ponderosa, for pine tip moth.

* Deadhead lilacs after they finish blooming. (See How-To Tip on page 112.)

MAY
MAINTENANCE TIPS

When ornamental grass is cut back, the plant loses some nutrients. Apply an organic or inorganic fertilizer (label should read 1–2–1 or something close) at the rate of one to two pounds per 1,000 square feet. Ornamental grasses should be planted with the top of the root ball slightly above the ground. They can be planted from now until the end of the growing season in September. Do not transplant ornamental grasses after the middle of July. If the container is two gallons (#2) or larger, plant the grass as you would a shrub. (See How-To Tip on page 120.) If smaller than two gallons, plant as you would a perennial.

MAY
MAINTENANCE TIPS

....

....

....

....

....

....

....

When you plant annuals, dig individual holes for plants in amended soil. (See How–To Tip on page 127.) Pinch (see How–To Tip on page 112) any blooms, make sure the plant and roots are wet, remove the container, and plant in the hole at the same depth as it was in the container or slightly higher in heavy clay soil. Disrupt the roots to stimulate and encourage them to grow out instead of circling in the ground. The label or seed package should tell you what type of location the plant will need (sun, shade, partial sun/shade), and how far apart to plant. Soak the ground around the plant thoroughly and mulch. (See How–To Tip on page 115.) The best time to plant is on a cool day or early in the morning or evening.

❋ Using a hand pruner, clip back new candles on evergreens to maintain compact growth. (See How-To Tip on page 119.)

❋ Mulch around trees and shrubs. (See How-To Tip on page 115.)

ROSES

❋ Fertilize your rose bushes. (See How-To Tip on page 114.)

❋ In higher elevations, prune back rose bushes and remove mounding that remains. (See How-To Tip on page 119.)

❋ Plant container roses after the last frost. (See How-To Tip on page 118.)

LAWN

❋ Check Lawn Maintenance Calendar. (See page 150.)

❋ Seed any dead areas in your lawn caused by disease or insects. (See page 54.)

❋ Fertilize warm season grasses in lower elevations and cool season grasses in higher elevations.

* Mow lawn to no less than 2" and never cut any more than one-third of the growth in a single cutting.

* If needed, apply broadleaf weed killer on the lawn either with a drop spreader or by spot spraying.

KITCHEN GARDEN

* Plant a salsa garden.

A salsa garden is easy to grow. Here are some ideas:

The plants in a typical salsa garden are chile peppers (your choice for flavor and heat – see page 148), roma tomatoes, onions, garlic, tomatillos, cilantro, basil, Mexican oregano, and parsley.

Grow all the ingredients and make your own combinations of salsa.

As a general rule, for every jalapeno or chile plant, you will need one tomato plant.

You can freeze, can, or serve your salsa fresh.

* Purchase vegetable transplants and seeds for direct sowing.

MAY
MAINTENANCE TIPS

Brown needles on pine trees can mean problems with insects or disease. However, pine trees, like deciduous trees, do periodically shed their needles. (Usually this occurs in the fall.) Typically, the inside needles that are older don't receive enough light to produce energy for the tree. They turn brown and eventually drop, while the newer needles on the outside of the tree remain green and continue to photosynthesize. If your needles are turning brown at the tips, or if entire branches are turning brown, you may have insects or a disease. Call your local garden center or arborist.

MAY
MAINTENANCE TIPS

....

....

....

....

....

....

....

Here's a vote for planting zinnias from seed. Zinnias will grow in average soil. They don't need lots of water. They come in all sizes and in about six colors. They like the sun and areas with good air circulation. They will bloom from early summer to late September. Zinnias are, in short, a flower made for our area. (Don't plant the larger, later-blooming varieties in higher elevations because they flower too late in the season.) Do not overhead sprinkle zinnias to reduce the chances for powdery mildew.

Have problems with rabbits? Here are some ideas:

Surround the garden or individual plants with chicken wire, leaving no openings. Bury the wire at least 4" into the soil.

Apply blood meal around the base of the plant. (Repeat after watering.)

Make a mixture of cayenne pepper (a little goes a long way) and water and spray on the plants. (This remedy needs to be repeated, especially if it snows or rains.)

Get a dog or cat.

❊ Plant radishes (in higher elevations), cucumbers, zucchini, and beans from seed. Reseed beans every few weeks to extend their harvest.

❊ If you want pumpkins by Halloween, plant the seeds now.

❊ Plant tomatoes and peppers from transplants (or seeds in lower elevations). Check the list on page 148 for the best varieties of chile peppers to grow in New Mexico.

❊ From transplants, plant herbs like basil, parsley, and chives. Try growing dill from seed.

MAY
MAINTENANCE TIPS

✳ From transplants, plant flowers such as marigolds and nasturtiums in the paths, between rows, and around the perimeter of the kitchen garden.

Want to keep your kitchen garden free of diseases, pests and weeds? Here are some ideas:

Select healthy transplants that are stocky and have not flowered or set fruit.

Interplant flowers and herbs throughout a kitchen garden to help distract and confuse insect pests throughout the summer.

Mulch garden pathways with old newspapers covered with straw or grass clippings. DO NOT use clippings treated with herbicides. Because newspapers might leach aluminum, use only a thin layer and keep it away from edible plants.

Don't over–crowd your plants. Air circulation is important, and disease is less likely to spread.

If you keep your garden clean, you can help minimize disease. Immediately throw away diseased plants, and old, unpicked vegetables. Don't add diseased material to the compost pile.

✳ Begin harvesting spring-planted cool season vegetables like peas, lettuce, spinach, and broccoli. (See How-To Tip on page 116.)

If you are growing tomatoes for the first time, start by purchasing the more common varieties found in garden centers: Early Girl, Better Boy, Champion, Celebrity, Ace, Sweet 100, Big Boy, Yellow Pear, San Marzano, and Roma VF. Harden off the plants for a few days on a porch or protected area outside, then plant in prepared soil in the full sun. Plant up to the first set of leaves, and follow the tag for spacing between plants. Place extra–large cages around the tomatoes after the second week. (The tomatoes will eventually grow into them.) Tomatoes need plenty of water and consistently warm weather. The soil must be kept evenly moist to produce the best fruit.

MAY
MAINTENANCE TIPS

....

....

....

....

....

....

....

There are some varieties of climbing vines that grow well in New Mexico: Virginia creeper, silverlace, English ivy, wisteria (in lower elevations), clematis, honeysuckle, woodbine, Boston ivy, grape, and hop. Trellis climbing vines for show, easier maintenance, and to keep them from crowding out other plants, trees, and shrubs. Allow for airflow on trellises near buildings, especially on the hot south or west exposures. (Do not allow vines to climb the sides of wood houses or fences because they can cause structural damage, which leads to rot.)

INTERIOR PLANTS

✳ This is a good month to divide and take cuttings from interior plants.

✳ In new potting soil, repot poinsettias that you plan to set outdoors in July. After repotting, cut the stems back to within 4" of the soil.

GENERAL

✳ Plant climbing vines in the early part of this month for great results the rest of the summer.

If you get frustrated with insect problems in your garden, here are some ideas:

Ladybugs and lacewings both serve as natural predators against a variety of different kinds of harmful insects in the garden. You can buy the larvae of both at a local garden center or you can check the Internet for sources.

Plants like carrots, mints, and daisies all attract beneficial insects to your garden.

Control aphids by getting rid of any ants.

Try a strong stream of water to get rid of harmful insects on your plants. If that doesn't work, you can either pick the larger pests off by hand, or check the How–To section on page 129.

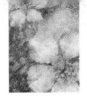

- ✳ Replenish organic mulches. (See How-To Tip on page 115.)

- ✳ Design and build a rock garden.

- ✳ Check your garden throughout the growing season for insects.

- ✳ Continue to weed your garden before weeds get too big or too numerous. (See How-To Tip on page 123.)

- ✳ Keep small stones swept off patios and walkways for safety reasons.

- ✳ Water your plants, trees, shrubs, and lawn infrequently, but thoroughly. (See How-To Tip on page 124.)

- ✳ Turn the compost pile. (See How-To Tip on page 111.)

MAY
MAINTENANCE TIPS

Rock gardens often look their best when displayed on a "berm." A berm is a raised area created by the mounding of fill dirt and smooth grading prior to soil preparation, boulder placement, and planting. If you have a flat landscape and don't want to put in a berm, large rocks, when grouped and set into the ground, will give the illusion of a raised area. For the most natural look, use rocks that come from your geographic area. If you bring in boulders, they should be buried to one-third their size into the grade. Otherwise, they will look unnatural. Generally, rock gardens do best in sunny areas.

SUMMER

June, July, August

JUNE
MAINTENANCE TIPS

....

....

....

....

....

....

....

If you don't divide bulbs like tulips, crocus, and hyacinths every three to five years, they will crowd each other out. Overcrowding with some bulbs can result in very small flowers. Other bulbs, like daffodils, actually tend to get bigger and better each year. Only divide them if they are getting overcrowded. Dig up a clump of the bulbs just after the foliage of the plant starts to turn yellow. (Make sure you dig deep enough to get the roots.) Then break off the bulbs from one another and either replant or store in a dry place until the fall. Do not cut off the foliage from the bulb even after you've divided them.

PERENNIALS/ ANNUALS/ BULBS

❋ Deadhead flowers as they fade to promote continuous bloom. (See How-To Tip on page 112.)

❋ Continue to plant summer flowering bulbs, like cannas, dahlias, and gladiolus. (Plant a few gladiolus each week for continuous blooms throughout the summer.)

❋ Note places in your landscape that could be filled next year with spring bulbs. Plant in the fall.

❋ Divide spring bulbs as the foliage dies. (See box this page.)

❋ Fertilize annuals and perennials with nitrogen-based fertilizer.

❋ In early June, continue planting herbs and annuals in containers for your porches, window boxes, patios, and decks.

❋ Plant annuals in containers and set in bare spots in your landscape. (You can get some good bargains on annuals now.)

Want to brighten up your landscape? Annuals planted in containers and set into or planted directly into your garden will do the job. Here are some ideas:

Find out how much sun your annuals will need before you decide where to plant them. If you put shade–loving annuals in a sunny area the plants will suffer!

Decide what height you will need before you plant your containers. You may need plants that add height for the back of a garden, or some that are shorter for the front edge of a border.

Plant annuals using good potting soil, in containers that drain well.

Some annuals must be pinched back to stay looking good all summer. (See How–To Tip on page 112.) If you don't want to spend the time, don't plant these kinds of annuals.

Here are some annuals you might not have thought of: coleus (provides beautiful texture and color), flowering tobacco (great scent and comes in a variety of heights and colors), gazania (drought–tolerant flowers), heliotrope (very Victorian with a nice scent and clustered flowers), and cleome (showy and tall).

JUNE
MAINTENANCE TIPS

Geraniums can be overwintered and then set outside for summer enjoyment. They tend to grow long, sparse stems if they are not cut back periodically. With pruners, cut stems about 2" to 3" from where they connect to another stem. To propagate new transplants, leave the tip of the stem and cut down about 5", just below one of the lines running around the stem. Dip the cut end into a rooting hormone for a few minutes. Plant the cuttings about 1 1/2" deep and the width of the cut stems. Keep the soil moist until they root. (The transplants can be moved outdoors but don't move the "mother" plant outside for a few weeks.)

JUNE
MAINTENANCE TIPS

....

....

....

....

....

....

....

There are many creative ways to plant containers for your porch, deck, patio, or window box. Seed an annual grass for a nice base for the rest of the flowers (don't overdo the amount). Lettuce makes a great filler plant. Plant strawberries in hanging baskets. In large containers, plant a miniature rock garden with rocks of different shapes and sizes and plants like dianthus, allium, campanula, and sedum. Or, grow water lilies and Japanese iris in an old lined wooden trough or half barrel. A combination of pansies, golden sage, and peppermint looks great. Surround small chile pepper plants with oregano or sage. If your creative juices refuse to flow, simply copy what your local garden center has done!

TREES AND SHRUBS

⁑ Make sure trees and shrubs are getting enough water this month.

ROSES

⁑ Fertilize rose bushes after the first round of flowers has started to die. (See How-To Tip on page 114.)

⁑ Cut back suckers from rose bushes. (See page 36.)

⁑ If the spring has been a wet one, watch for black spot and powdery mildew. (See How-To Tip on page 129.)

LAWN

⁑ Check the Lawn Maintenance Calendar. (See page 150.)

⁑ Check drip and lawn system. Remove any emitters that are clogged or overwatering and add emitters to areas where the soil is dry. (See How-To Tip on page 124.)

⁑ Seed or sod warm season grasses like blue gramma and buffalograss.

⁑ Mow lawn to no less than 2" and never cut any more than one-third of the growth in a single cutting.

⁑ Watch lawns on south and west faces for drought stress.

KITCHEN GARDEN

❋ Water seeds and transplants daily after planting. Do this for two weeks to keep the soil moist and allow seeds to germinate.

❋ Shade new transplants between 10 a.m. and 4 p.m. the first week they are planted if daytime temperatures exceed 92°. Gradually introduce the plants to the sun.

❋ Finish harvesting spring-planted cool season vegetables such as peas, lettuce, and spinach.

❋ Look for radishes planted in May to be ready toward the end of this month.

❋ It's not too late to plant many vegetables, especially in lower elevations. Check the number of growing days for particular varieties.

❋ Watch for caterpillars on crops and treat with Bt (see page 129), or pick them off and cover plants with row covers.

❋ Plant vegetable gardens and bedding plants early this month at higher elevations.

JUNE
MAINTENANCE TIPS

If you have a rose bush that now produces some roses that are different than what they were originally, check the bush carefully. If it still has any branches growing from the graft, the bush will continue to grow as the original if you remove the suckers with the different roses below the graft. If all the suckers are growing from the roots or below the graft, the bush will not grow the original roses again. (To avoid this problem, ask at your garden center for roses grown on their own roots.)

JUNE
MAINTENANCE TIPS

....

....

....

....

....

....

....

This month is a good time to assess how much water your gardens are getting. Remember that garden beds need, on average, 2" of water per week, and it's preferable to water deeply and less frequently. (Lawns need about 1" of water per week, on average.) Set margarine cups out in five or six areas in your garden beds. Measure and mark ½" and 1" from the bottom on the side of the cup. Start your water source (irrigation system, drip emitters, sprinkler) and check the cups in 20 minutes. You will then be able to tell how long you need to run the source to water each area the proper amount each week. You can also then see which areas are getting too much water and which are not getting enough.

INTERIOR PLANTS

✳ Thoroughly clean all indoor plants. (See How-To Tip on page 111.)

✳ Wash out or replace all plant saucers to get rid of salt build-up.

GENERAL

✳ Check for diseases or insects that may be attacking plants. (See How-To Tip on page 129.)

✳ Weed your garden once a week. (See How-To Tip on page 123.) Stop using herbicides on weeds at this time and remove with a hoe or by hand, etc. (Many herbicides, when used to control weeds in hot summer weather, can cause injury to nearby healthy plants.)

✳ Keep small stones swept off patios and walkways for safety reasons.

✳ This month can be extremely hot and windy with high light intensity. Check for extra water needs and plant protection. (See How-To Tips on pages 115 and 124.)

✳ Turn the compost pile once every two weeks during this month. (See How-To Tip on page 111.)

PERENNIALS/ ANNUALS/ BULBS

❋ Continue to pinch, cut, and deadhead perennials and annuals.

❋ Pinch mums only until the end of the month, then stop for better fall flowers.

❋ Divide and replant Oriental poppies after the foliage begins to die.

❋ Create an environment with plants that will attract hummingbirds.

❋ Create an environment with plants that will attract butterflies. (See page 39.)

Want to build a home for butterflies? Here are a few ideas:

Because it can get windy, plant your butterfly garden in an area that is sheltered or enclosed. Trees and shrubs work, as do fences, or a trellis with a flowering vine.

Butterflies will perch in shrubs, tree crevices, under bark, or in log piles.

Because butterflies like heat, having rocks and evergreens in your garden will help attract them. (Rocks and evergreens absorb the sun.)

JULY
MAINTENANCE TIPS

If you want to attract hummingbirds to your garden, remember that they like sunny areas, red or orange objects, and shapes that are tubular (for their long, tube–like tongue). Because they need to be able to see the plants from a long distance (at least 30 feet overhead) colors should be vivid to catch their attention. If you want to attract both butterflies and hummingbirds, plant separate gardens so they don't compete with one another. Some of the plants hummingbirds like best are flowering crabapple trees, clematis, verbena, geraniums, bee balm, phlox, sweet William, coral bells, morning glories, gladiolus, and dianthus.

JULY

....

....

....

....

....

....

....

If you want to attract butterflies to your garden, remember they like bright, damp areas with flat stones or boards where they can sun themselves. You first must create an environment that is healthy for the butterfly caterpillar, then one that attracts the adult butterfly. Plants necessary for butterfly caterpillars are wild lupine, wild asters, goldenrod, statice, parsley, and dill. (They also like milkweed, thistle, clover, etc., but these weeds aren't always compatible with other garden goals.) Some of the plants butterflies like best are petunia, marigold, foxglove, impatiens, cosmos, verbena, snapdragon, strawberry, bee balm, daylily, black–eyed Susan, coreopsis, and liatris.

Fill a container with sand and saturate it with water. (Butterflies can't drink from open water.)

✽ Watch for tobacco budworm, which feeds on flower buds of petunias, geraniums and flowering tobacco. Pick off or treat these tiny caterpillars with Bt (see page 129) as soon as you find them.

TREES AND SHRUBS

✽ Do not use high nitrogen fertilizer on trees from now until next March.

✽ Make sure trees and shrubs are getting enough water during the hottest months. (See How-To Tip on page 124.)

✽ To produce larger fruit, thin the tiny fruits on your trees to a hand-span between each.

✽ Watch for insect outbreaks on newly planted trees.

ROSES

✽ Keep an eye on rose leaves for black spot and powdery mildew. Treat if necessary. (See How-To Tip on page 129.)

* Deadhead roses after they bloom. (See How-To Tip on page 112.)

* Fertilize roses. (See How-To Tip on page 114.)

LAWN

* Check Lawn Maintenance Calendar. (See page 150.)

* Non-treated grass makes a good mulch in vegetable garden pathways and around plants.

* Avoid fertilizer that is high in nitrogen when temperatures are hot. (You can use slow-release nitrogen.)

* Mow the lawn to no less than 2" in height, never cutting more than one-third of the growth in a single mowing.

* Resharpen lawn mower blades.

* Hot, south-facing lawns need extra water because they dry out quickly in summer.

* Lawns with excessive thatch (greater than ½") may need extra water.

* During the hottest parts of the summer, lawns should get approximately 2" of water per week instead of the normal 1" per week at other times.

JULY
MAINTENANCE TIPS

Too much thatch in your lawn isn't healthy because it prevents movement of air and water to the root zone of your grass. Thatch is a spongy, organic layer composed of grass roots, stems, and other dark organic materials. When you have a lot of thatch, grass roots will grow in the thatch, not the soil. Because thatch doesn't hold water, the lawn can dry out more easily than normal, especially in cold weather or hot temperatures. Aerating the lawn can help since removing plugs of soil will increase air circulation. This increases decomposition of the thatch.

JULY
MAINTENANCE TIPS

....

....

....

....

....

....

....

There are a number of flowers you can grow that are good to eat. (Usually it's the petals you eat, not the stems or the centers of the flowers.) When you cook with edible flowers, use only petals that you know are home–grown and haven't been treated with chemicals. There are a number of ways to prepare petals: dip in batter and deep fry, add to soups and salads, steam in stir fry, stuff and bake, use to make tea, or add as a garnish. For sweet eating, make candied flowers. Some of the more common edible flowers include squash and pumpkin blossoms, roses, daylilies, tulips, pansies, borage, nasturtiums, dianthus, scented geraniums, and chrysanthemums.

KITCHEN GARDEN

❋ Make sure the garden is well-mulched to protect plants during the heat of the day. Keep heat-loving weeds under control. (See How-To Tip on page 123.)

❋ Begin harvesting the first tomatoes around mid-July.

❋ Begin harvesting cool season vegetables and herbs in the higher elevations. (See How-To Tip on page 116.)

❋ Pull spring-planted cool season vegetables that are finished producing. Add the plants to the compost pile.

❋ Many cool season vegetables can be planted this month for fall harvesting. Peas, cabbage, and lettuce are not only tolerant of frost, but their flavor actually improves after a light frost. (See page 116.)

❋ Watch for grasshoppers if the weather has been hot and dry.

❋ Watch for slugs and snails if the weather has been cooler and wet. (See How-To Tip on page 129.)

INTERIOR PLANTS

✳ Poinsettias that still have their leaves can be set outside.

Poinsettias are nice additions to the summer garden. Here are a few tips:

Help your poinsettia acclimate to the outdoors by putting it in a shady area, like a porch, for a week or so.

It is recommended that you leave the poinsettia in the pot when you move it outdoors. You can either plant the pot, or set the poinsettia in and among other plants and flowers in your garden.

Place or plant the pot in a lightly shaded area.

Water so that the soil in the pot is moist, but not soggy.

Remove 1" off each stem in August, so the plant stays short and stocky.

✳ Watch that houseplants are not in the direct sun to protect tender leaves from burning.

GENERAL

✳ Spider mites really begin to emerge this month, so keep in touch with your plants, trees, and shrubs and treat when necessary. (See How-To Tip on page 129.)

JULY
MAINTENANCE TIPS

There are several ways to help cut flowers last longer. First, cut your flowers before mid–morning. The stems should be cut at an angle and immediately put into a bucket of water. Use sharp shears. Once inside, do your trim work with the stems under water. The stems of roses and poppies should be plunged into boiling water first and then transferred into their permanent vase or container. Get rid of any leaves that will be submerged. If you add floral food, you only need to change the water every two days. If not, change the water daily and keep cutting ½" from the stems each time you change the water. Don't place the arrangement in or very near the sun or in warm areas.

JULY
MAINTENANCE TIPS

....

....

....

....

....

....

....

Spider mites like our hot, dry weather in June, July, August, and part of September. A possible sign of spider mites is fine webbing on plants. The leaves or needles on evergreen trees will turn dull green/yellow, and appear speckled. Red "speckles" may move on the underside of leaves. You want to treat spider mites because they have the ability to go dormant during cold weather, only to return when it gets warm again. Lacewings are the natural enemies of spider mites. If you haven't seen many in your garden, ask your local garden center if they sell any lacewing eggs or larvae or check the Internet for sources. If lacewings don't do the job, look for other remedies on page 129.

❊ If you cut woody-stemmed branches (such as forsythia or lilacs) to put in an arrangement, hit several inches of the bottoms of the stems with a hammer before putting in water.

❊ Continue to weed your garden. (See How-To Tip on page 123.) Watch to see that weeds don't grow so large that they flower and drop seeds. (This creates more weeds!)

❊ Keep up with watering needs in your garden. Even though we can get frequent afternoon showers, the amount of moisture can be deceiving. These storms rarely produce enough water to soak the soil and benefit your plants. (See How-To Tip on page 124.)

❊ Keep small stones swept off patios and walkways for safety reasons.

❊ Turn the compost pile twice this month. (See How-To Tip on page 111.)

PERENNIALS/ ANNUALS/ BULBS

✳ Continue to deadhead, pinch, and cut annuals and perennials. (See How-To Tip on page 112.)

✳ Pinch back spindly annuals and fertilize for another spurt of growth. (See page 45.)

✳ Divide bearded iris bulbs in early August.

✳ Select and cut flowers, grasses, and leaves that you want to dry for display in arrangements.

TREES AND SHRUBS

✳ Remove evergreen branches that are dead or diseased. (See How-To Tip on page 119.)

✳ Do not fertilize trees and shrubs until next spring.

✳ Make sure trees and shrubs get enough water during August.

ROSES

✳ Last month to fertilize rose bushes. Do not fertilize after the middle of the month.

✳ Stop deadheading roses so they can begin to harden off and form rose hips.

AUGUST
MAINTENANCE TIPS

The feel and colors of spring, summer, and fall can all be kept alive by drying your favorite flowers, grasses, and leaves. Gather the stems together and secure with a rubber band. Hang upside down in a warm, dark room or area until the stems become brittle. Store the finished dried plants in paper bags.

AUGUST
MAINTENANCE TIPS

....

....

....

....

....

....

....

Annuals tend to have a pause in growth in August. To pep them up, cut the stems back by at least half, use an organic fertilizer in the soil around them, and soak the plant and soil thoroughly. You can also fertilize with a 5–10–5 fertilizer, or a water soluble fertilizer.

❊ Watch for powdery mildew on roses, flowers, and squash. Water early in the day to help prevent mildew.

LAWN

❊ Check Lawn Maintenance Calendar. (See page 150.)

❊ For lower elevations, this is the last month you can install warm season grasses.

❊ Mow lawn to no less than 2 ½" and never cut any more than one-third of the growth.

❊ Pay particular attention to good watering practices this month. Stressed areas in the full sun, or on southern or western slopes may need extra watering.

KITCHEN GARDEN

❊ Continue harvesting tomatoes, warm season vegetables, and herbs. (See How-To Tip on page 116.)

Want to use the herbs you grow as seasonings in your food? Here are some ideas:

Basil tastes good in tomatoes, herb oil, vinaigrettes, Italian dishes, egg and cheese dishes, and with rosemary in bread.

Chives can be used with sour cream for a dip, in egg dishes, potato dishes, in vegetable seasonings, and in Mexican dishes.

Dill is great in salads, dips, dressings, with fish, on tomatoes, in egg dishes, and in chicken dishes.

Mint is good in tea, lemonade, and other fresh drinks.

Oregano is good in stews, soups, and Italian dishes.

Parsley is a good garnish, but it can also be used in almost any main course, salad, or soup dish. It's also good in egg and cheese dishes.

Rosemary can be used in breads, chicken dishes, pork dishes, and in vinaigrettes.

Sage can be used in Italian dishes, turkey stuffing, and vegetable seasonings.

Thyme is good in turkey stuffing, on vegetables and tomatoes, and in stews.

✳ Begin to harvest beans, peppers, and cucumbers. (See How-To Tip on page 116.)

✳ Harvest garlic in lower elevations.

✳ Plants used to make salsa may be ready for harvest. (See How-To tip on page 116.)

AUGUST
MAINTENANCE TIPS

What to do with all those chile peppers you've grown? Make a ristra! Ristras are the long, hanging decorations that are made from chile peppers. Pick the chile pods when they are red or starting to turn red (usually this month). To make a 3–foot–long ristra, you will need about ¾ of a bushel of chile peppers. Tie three chile peppers together by wrapping cotton string around the stems. Then tie the group to a piece of twine. Do this with a series of sets of three chile peppers, tying the groups onto the main piece of twine 3" to 4" apart. At the top of the twine, tie a piece of looped wire so you can hang the ristra. Hang the ristra outside in a cool, dry, airy place until it is completely dry.

AUGUST
MAINTENANCE TIPS

- ✻ Plant cool season vegetables now for fall harvesting. (See page 116.)
- ✻ Make certain plants are watered adequately on hot August days.
- ✻ Watch for pests like cabbage butterflies and tomato hornworms. (See page 48.)
- ✻ Watch for spider mites on tomatoes and peppers. Hose off with insecticidal soap in early morning. (See How-To Tip on page 129.)
- ✻ Share produce with your local food bank.
- ✻ Zucchini puree is great for the compost pile when you run out of friends and neighbors to give your zucchini to!

GENERAL

- ✻ Create a garden "Junkyard."

Every garden has plants that just don't seem to perform or do well, regardless of your best efforts. Instead of waiting until the plant dies, try transplanting it into your "Junkyard," the "I don't know what else to do with it" catch-all garden. Here are some ideas:

Plan your Junkyard for an area that isn't seen by others. (Don't put it in front of your house!)

After mid-August, do not fertilize woody, flowering shrubs like rose bushes. You don't want to continue to stimulate more growth than necessary. This way, the shrubs will be encouraged to harden off before the first freeze.

Take special care to amend the soil properly (see How–To Tip on page 127), and to make sure the garden has a good source for water. (Since this garden is a last–ditch effort, you might as well give the plants the best chance possible!)

Note, throughout the growing season, which plants are not doing well. Move them quickly into the Junkyard.

Make sure that the problem with the plant isn't insects or disease. (If this is what you suspect, treat the plant, don't move it. See How–To Tip on page 129.)

You can put more than plants in your Junkyard. How about broken pottery to form a pathway? Or old furniture planted over with vines?

AUGUST
MAINTENANCE TIPS

* Pay special attention to find insect and disease problems this month.

* Weed your garden frequently.

* Make sure plants in the garden are getting adequate water this month.

* Start a compost pile with leftovers from the garden. (See How-To Tip on page 111.)

Tomato hornworms are green caterpillars that are three to five inches long and have black horns on their rear ends. The easiest remedy is to pick them off by hand (sometimes hard to do, considering their looks). Spraying with Bt (Bacillus thuringiensis) usually is effective and safe to use on edible plants. If you see white cocoons on the back of the hornworm, leave them alone because these hold parasitic wasps (the natural enemy of the hornworm) who are doing their job. Another suggestion for cooler mountain gardens is to plant tomatoes in plastic containers because pests like the hornworm can't easily climb the slick sides of the pot.

FALL

September, October, November

SEPTEMBER
MAINTENANCE TIPS

....

....

....

....

....

....

....

There are a number of bulbs you can buy to plant in the fall for spring blooming: daffodils, tulips (hybrid tulips will die out after a few seasons), lilies, snowdrops, crocus, and hyacinth. All of these fall bulbs can be left in the ground for years. They do not need to be dug up in the fall, unlike bulbs planted in the spring that bloom in the summer. They should, however, be divided periodically. (See page 33.) When you buy bulbs, buy them big, regardless of the type. If the bulbs are slightly mushy, soft, or dried up don't buy them. If they look damaged, don't buy them. Buying bulbs on sale might be risky, especially if they're small.

PERENNIALS/ ANNUALS/ BULBS

❊ Choose any annuals you want to overwinter now and pot them. At higher elevations, bring inside before a frost and set near a sunny window or in a greenhouse. Be sure to disinfect any of the plants before you bring them inside. (See page 76.)

❊ Transplant and/or divide peonies if necessary. (Caution: Peonies hate to be moved!) (See page 52.)

❊ Transplant and/or divide spring and summer-blooming perennials (but not fall perennials). (See page 19.)

❊ Plant new perennials.

❊ Plant pansies, violas, and mums for fall color.

❊ Sow seed for self-seeding annuals like California poppies, love-in-a-mist, and cosmos.

❊ Divide daylilies now. (See page 19.)

❊ Plant ground covers.

SEPTEMBER
MAINTENANCE TIPS

❋ Purchase bulbs for fall planting. (You can either buy from garden centers or from mail order catalogs.) (See page 51.) Wait until October to plant.

❋ Consider collecting and saving seeds from your flowers and vegetables to plant in your garden next year.

How do you collect seeds from your favorite plants? Here are some ideas:

Mark the plants that you want to gather seed from so you don't accidentally pick all the blooms. You'll know when the pods are ready because they will become dry but won't have opened and scattered their seed. (Rarely do all the pods on one plant open at the same time, so even if the first few pods open, you'll still be able to gather plenty.)

If the pod is fragile, cover it with a paper bag (tie it at the bottom of the pod) before it gets dry.

After you have gathered the seeds from the pods, air dry them for a week. Store them in airtight containers in a cool, dry place. (Mark the containers with the names of the plants.)

❋ Fall cleanup takes place in the higher elevations this month. Cut down all dry perennials and water them thoroughly. Compost or discard all annuals and bedding plants.

To transplant and/or divide peonies, dig up the entire plant, making sure to get all the roots. At the crown of each plant, there will be pink buds. Use a knife to divide the plant so there are no more than three buds in each division. Dig a hole in amended soil, (see How–To Tip on page 127) and plant your divided peonies close to the surface, covering the buds with only 1" of soil. Water well after transplanting. Peonies like sunny locations that drain well.

SEPTEMBER
MAINTENANCE TIPS

....

....

....

....

....

....

....

This month is a good time to remove grass that grows right up to the trunks of trees. Dig out the grass (or use glyphosate, but don't get any on the tree or tree suckers). Once the grass is dead, put down mulch, such as wood chips, where the grass has been removed. This needs to be done so that when mowers or weed-eaters are used, the tree trunk isn't damaged. (If you keep hitting the trunk with lawn equipment, the tree may eventually die.)

TREES AND SHRUBS

❋ Plant or transplant evergreens from one location in the garden to another before the weather turns cool. (See How-To Tip on page 120.)

❋ Harvest pears before they ripen on the tree. (Pears picked green have better flavor.)

❋ Do not fertilize trees and shrubs now.

ROSES

❋ Stop deadheading and let rose hips form. The rose plant will now begin to harden off for the winter.

LAWN

❋ Check Lawn Maintenance Calendar. (See page 150.)

❋ Mow lawn to 2" and never cut any more than one-third of the growth in a single cutting.

❋ Reseed parts of lawn that need it. (See page 54.)

❋ Winterize irrigation systems in higher elevations. (See page 58.)

❋ In higher elevations, apply winterizer fertilizer on the lawn and aerate.

✻ Install cool season grasses.

KITCHEN GARDEN

✻ Continue harvesting cucumbers, beans, zucchini, and other vegetables from the garden. [See How-To Tip on page 116.]

✻ Harvest all green tomatoes before the first frost. They will turn red after removal from the plants. [See How-To Tip on page 116.]

✻ Harvest cabbage, carrots, and brussel sprouts after the first mild frost (32°). [See How-To Tip on page 116.]

✻ Harvest garlic. Save some of the ripest cloves for replanting in October. [See How-To Tip on page 116.]

✻ Harvest and dry herbs.

If you don't plan to have an inside herb garden during the winter, dry those from your garden to use until next spring. Here are some ideas:

Cut the herbs in the mid–morning to help preserve the flavors in the herbs. Trim off up to one–third of the plant to use for drying. Don't chop the herbs up before drying.

SEPTEMBER
MAINTENANCE TIPS

Spring and summer activities can be hard on grass. Bare spots caused by disease, insects, dogs, kids, and mower scalping can be corrected by reseeding. With a garden fork, stab the soil in the bare spot and then rake the area. Spread the seed with your hand (avoid a windy day), using 1 ounce per square yard of the same seed as the rest of your lawn. Lightly cover the seed with amended soil from another part of the yard and use a hoe to lightly compress the soil. (Don't bury the seed totally.) Water with a fine spray and keep the soil damp (not wet) until germination, which should occur one to two weeks after planting. Then water on the same schedule as the rest of the lawn.

SEPTEMBER
MAINTENANCE TIPS

....

....

....

....

....

....

....

Poinsettias that have been saved from the previous year have lost their red, coral, or white colors by now. Start placing the plants in a cool, dark place for 14 hours at night (approximately 5 p.m. until 7 a.m.). Expose them to the light during the day. Repeat this process every day until the plant's bracts (uppermost leaves) turn color. Depending on the variety, your poinsettia will bloom after eight to eleven weeks. The poinsettia should be colorful just in time for the holiday season.

When air–drying, tie the herbs together in bundles, put in a paper bag that has holes punched in the sides, put a rubber band around the top, and hang upside down. For best results, dry indoors.

You can also dry herbs in a cool oven by layering the leaves (not touching) between layers of paper towels. The light in the oven should be enough to dry the herbs out overnight.

Store herbs in airtight containers away from heat and away from light. (Don't store them above or near the oven or stove.)

INTERIOR PLANTS

✳ Bring indoors any poinsettias that were set out for the summer. Near the end of the month, begin to put them in a dark, cool, dry place for 14 hours so the bracts will turn color.

GENERAL

✳ Watch for predictions of early frosts at higher elevations. Cover plants if necessary. Pull container plants indoors, cover plants in gardens with bed sheets, newspapers, paper bags, blankets, burlap, or row covers. (Don't use plastic.)

✳ Turn the compost pile.

PERENNIALS/ ANNUALS/ BULBS

✳ Seed your wildflower garden now for spring blooming.

Seeding a wildflower garden isn't difficult! Here are some ideas:

The garden will need at least partial sun, preferably full sun.

Prepare the soil as you would for any other garden. (See How–To Tip on page 127.) Make sure to get rid of any weeds or grasses.

Mix the seed with organic material like peat to provide an even distribution.

Spread the wildflower mix evenly across the prepared soil surface, going back and forth in one direction, such as north to south. Repeat this at a perpendicular angle to the area you just sowed, such as east to west.

Rake the seed in no deeper than ¼". Then tap down the seed so the soil is firm.

Water your wildflower garden on a regular basis so that the ground stays damp until the seeds germinate. Then water once a week, or when the garden needs it.

✳ Bring in any pots of tender perennials that you plan to overwinter.

OCTOBER
MAINTENANCE TIPS

When you plant a wildflower garden in the fall, the seeds will overwinter. This means that the seeds will lay dormant until spring and then start to grow. While there is some risk of the seeds being eaten by birds or animals, don't sow more than the label indicates. The mix will contain enough seed to compensate. It's also not a good idea to over–seed because the early bloomers in the mix will squeeze out the later bloomers. Be prepared: In most mixes, some of the perennial flowers won't bloom until the second year. Which mix? Ask at your local garden center for the best mix for your area. If you don't want grasses planted with your wildflowers, check the label to make sure none are included in the mix.

OCTOBER
MAINTENANCE TIPS

....

....

....

....

....

....

....

Plant bulbs like tulips, hyacinths, daffodils, and crocuses in the fall for blooming next spring. The soil should be well amended (see How–To Tip on page 127), and add a little phosphorus at the bottom of the hole before planting. There is a limit to the number of bulbs that can be planted per square foot: tulips – 8 to 10, hyacinths and daffodils – 5, and crocuses – 10 to 15. Try planting in groupings among the perennials and shrubs. Pay attention to when they bloom (some bloom earlier or later than others) and heights, to help you orchestrate spring color.

❋ Plant new perennials. Apply a balanced organic fertilizer. (See How-To Tip on page 114.)

❋ Plant hardy bulbs for spring blooming. (See box this page.)

❋ Buy extra spring bulbs for forcing. (See page 65.)

❋ If you haven't already planted pansies, plant now, along with your spring flowering bulbs. In lower elevations, you can also plant ornamental kale.

❋ Dig up gladiolus, cannas, and dahlias when leaves begin to turn yellow. Store them for the winter. (See page 59.)

❋ Mulch around perennials after the second hard frost in the higher elevations. (It's too late for most rodents to nest and destroy roots.) (See How-To Tip on page 115.)

❋ Our fall is generally characterized by an early freeze followed by an Indian summer. To extend the season with color (and vegetables and herbs), use row covers.

TREES AND SHRUBS

❋ Continue watering all trees and shrubs until the first hard freeze (even if the leaves have changed color and fallen).

* Plant container and balled and burlapped trees and shrubs. (See How-To Tip on page 120.)

* Tree leaves and old fruit should be raked and composted, tilled into the garden, or used as mulch.

If you want to make mulch out of tree leaves, here are some ideas:

Only till or use as mulch if you're very sure the leaves are not diseased.

Chop the leaves up into small pieces so they will decompose more easily and won't blow away. You can do this by running over them with a mower.

Sprinkle slow–release nitrogen fertilizer on top of newly mulched beds. This will help soil and nutrients stay balanced.

* In higher elevations, wrap the trunks of all young and tender barked trees in mid-to-late October. (See page 63.)

* Do not fertilize trees and shrubs now.

ROSES

* Do not prune roses. Tie down tall branches far enough so they don't get buffeted by the wind.

OCTOBER
MAINTENANCE TIPS

It's necessary in higher elevations to "blow out" all the water in your sprinkler system each fall. This prevents the water lines from freezing and breaking during the winter. (Repair of irrigation lines is no fun.) Contact a sprinkler shop to come and do the job or rent the necessary equipment (compressor and proper attachments) at an equipment rental shop. Watch the weather, and if temperatures are due to drop below freezing, flush and drain your irrigation systems. Disconnect hoses, drain them, and bring them inside for the winter. If you leave them connected, outside faucets can be damaged.

OCTOBER
MAINTENANCE TIPS

....

....

....

....

....

....

....

....

We need to dig up and store certain flower bulbs over the winter (gladiolus, cannas, dahlias, and certain exotic daffodils). After digging, let the bulbs dry out for about one week and then store in packing material (peat moss, vermiculite, sand, sawdust) in a cool (about 50°), dry place. If the bulbs become diseased or start rotting, throw them out; if sprouting, move to a place that is colder and/or drier.

✻ Water when the soil is dry. (See How-To Tip on page 124.)

✻ Mulch shrub roses after the second hard frost in the higher elevations. (It's too late for most rodents to nest and destroy roots.) (See How-To Tip on page 115.)

LAWN

✻ Check Lawn Maintenance Calendar. (See page 150.)

✻ Apply a winterizing fertilizer on the lawn and aerate. (See page 114.)

✻ Rake dead leaves off the lawn.

✻ Mow for the last time in mid-October. Mow lawn to 2".

✻ If moisture is minimal, water your lawn.

✻ Winterize the irrigation system before a hard freeze, especially in higher elevations.

KITCHEN GARDEN

✻ Plant garlic cloves.

✻ Harvest brussel sprouts and pumpkins after the first frost. (See page 60.) (See How-To Tip on page 116.)

✻ Harvest winter squash and gourds. (See box on page 60.)

* Pull and compost finished vegetable plants. (See How-To Tip on page 111.)

* In higher elevations, spade vegetable garden and add organic matter such as finished compost.

* Put mulch around your carrots and other root crops to keep the ground from freezing. You can then continue to harvest for another couple of months.

INTERIOR PLANTS

* Thoroughly clean and prune back indoor plants. (See How-To Tip on page 111.)

GENERAL

* If you do have leaves and plant materials that you know or suspect are diseased, put them in a "hot" compost pile (140° to 160°) or discard.

Want to start a "hot" compost pile? Here are some ideas:

You can compost diseased plant materials in a hot pile; discard anything you suspect has insect problems.

OCTOBER
MAINTENANCE TIPS

Harvest winter squash and gourds. Cure in a warm (75° to 85°) dry place for 10 days. Then store in a cool (50° to 55°), dry location. Many will keep until early spring. Pumpkins are ready to harvest when they are orange in color, and the skin is hard. The rind should not be easily penetrated by a thumbnail. Harvesting can be done any time before a severe frost. When harvesting the pumpkin, leave several inches of stem on the stock.

OCTOBER
MAINTENANCE TIPS

....

....

....

....

....

....

....

Our state is known for our beautiful fall weather. Plants enjoy it also. Generally, the winds are mild, the temperatures are not extreme, and the humidity is higher than usual. The result is an ideal time to plant almost everything with the exception of some broadleaf evergreens, warm season grasses, and of course, annuals. The roots of plants planted now will have the opportunity to establish themselves and supply the leaves with much—needed moisture in the spring. This allows the plant a healthy start for an entire growing season.

Unlike a normal compost pile, you will use equal amounts of green materials (nitrogen) and brown materials (carbon) in the hot compost pile or bin. Sources of nitrogen can be found in leafy plants, vegetable garden waste, grass clippings, and kitchen waste. Sources of carbon can be found in leaves or shredded tree and shrub branches.

Layer your materials, starting with brown and followed by green, until the pile is about 4' tall. (The first layer should be branches or something that allows for good air circulation.)

Water the pile until it is moist (not wet!).

Monitor the temperature until it reaches approximately 140°, which will take anywhere from four to seven days. When the temperature begins to decrease, turn the pile, and the temperature will begin to rise again. Repeat this process once a week for two more weeks.

After turning the pile a third time, wait one more week and compost should be finished and ready to use.

✳ Water trees, shrubs, and roses if needed. (See How-To Tip on page 124.)

✳ Turn the compost pile. (See How-To Tip on page 111.)

PERENNIALS/ ANNUALS/ BULBS

❋ If you haven't already done so, mulch around plants. (See How-To Tip on page 115.)

❋ Check stored bulbs to make sure they aren't sprouting or rotting. (See page 59.)

❋ If the ground isn't frozen, you can still plant bulbs. (They may bloom a little later than those planted in September or October but they will still bloom.)

❋ Cut back perennials from last year so they will bloom better.

TREES AND SHRUBS

❋ Mulch young or newly planted trees and shrubs. (See How-To Tip on page 115.) Wait until the end of the month when the ground is frozen.

❋ Brush heavy snow off tree and shrub limbs in higher elevations.

NOVEMBER
MAINTENANCE TIPS

....

....

....

....

....

....

....

It's important to cut back perennials now. If the foliage is diseased, it will not only re–infect the plant next season but it also could spread the disease to other plants. With a sharp pair of pruners, remove dead plant material all the way to the crown. Remove or compost debris.

NOVEMBER
MAINTENANCE TIPS

....

....

....

....

....

....

....

Trees and shrubs that are exposed to the south or southwest are prone to sunscald in the winter. On sunny days, the temperatures in the sun can get as high as 60°, and, because the tree has no leaves for protection, the tender bark will freeze and then thaw, thus cracking. To prevent sunscald, wrap the tree trunk with tree wrap or any other light–colored material that can be removed in the spring. The trunk also can be sprayed with a diluted white latex (not oil–based) paint.

❋ Dig a hole for planting a live Christmas tree after the holiday season in December. (If you wait until after the holidays, the ground may be frozen and hard to work with.) Bag the soil from the hole and add soil amendments now, as well.

❋ Leave the snow on low-lying shrubs to act as an insulator in higher elevations.

❋ Check the guys, wiring, and stakes on all trees to make sure they are not girdling, pinching, or strangling the tree. Remember, tree straps should only be used temporarily after the tree is first planted. (See How-To Tip on page 122.)

❋ Wrap or whitewash the trunks of all young and tender barked trees. (See box this page.)

❋ Protect new trees and shrubs from deer, elk, or other wildlife.

Want to make sure your new trees and shrubs will survive the winter without getting eaten? If you don't want to fence, here are some ideas:

There are liquid substances that can be rubbed on trees and shrubs that taste bad to wildlife. The liquid is safe for both the wildlife and the plant (not for edible plants).

Tree grates come in a variety of styles, materials, and sizes.

Tree guards made of plastic tubing are usually effective. Plastic mesh tree guards can be used, but are not as effective as the tubing.

You can make your own protectors from chicken wire. If you do use wire, make sure to remove it carefully once the tree or shrub branches start to grow through.

ROSES

- ❊ Mulch rose bushes in early November or when the temperature in your yard has dropped to 22°.

LAWN

- ❊ Check Lawn Maintenance Calendar. (See page 150.)
- ❊ Clean and store away lawn tools and lawn mower.

Here are some ideas for cleaning and storing your garden tools:

Drain the gasoline out of all equipment or add a stabilizer.

Keep a mixture of three parts sand and one part motor oil handy to clean tools during and after the gardening season. The sand takes off dirt and debris; the oil prevents rusting.

Rinse out clay pots and put them where they won't freeze over the winter.

NOVEMBER
MAINTENANCE TIPS

To help rose bushes survive the winter temperature fluctuations, mound them with mulch such as soil, straw, or wood chips. (Don't use sawdust because it blocks winter watering.) The mulch should extend from the center of the bush out, 8" high, around all canes of the bush. (This mounding should be removed in late March or April.)

NOVEMBER
MAINTENANCE TIPS

....

....

....

....

....

....

....

Create a touch of spring during the cold winter months by "forcing" spring bulbs to grow in pots inside your home. Buy healthy tulip, hyacinth, daffodil, dwarf or Dutch iris, and crocus bulbs early this month. Set the bulbs close together in shallow pots in good potting soil. The tip of the bulb should be exposed by about one–third (iris should be covered). Water thoroughly, then place the pots in a cold location (consistent 40°) for 13 to 15 weeks. Check the bulbs to see if they have developed a number of roots; if they have, the bulbs are ready to "graduate" to a warmer location (consistent 55°). As growth shoots up, move the pots to a permanent location.

After use or cleaning, immediately put garden tools away to avoid injuries. Pegboard or hooks in the garage are a good idea.

✳ In higher elevations, winterize your irrigation system and drain your hoses if you haven't already done so. Do now before the pipes freeze or your outside faucets crack. (See page 58.)

KITCHEN GARDEN

✳ Harvest and store potatoes for use over the winter in early November.

You can store your potatoes to use over the winter. Here are some ideas:

Potatoes should only be harvested after the first fall frost. If you plan to store them, let the potatoes remain on the vine for two weeks before picking them.

First you need to let the potatoes "cure" by placing them in a pile in a dark area with good air circulation for at least seven days. The temperature should be 55° to 65°. (In lower elevations you can leave them in a pile in your garden and cover them with a piece of burlap, but protect them from rain.)

To store, place potatoes in a dark area that is fairly humid, and the temperature is 35° to 40°. (No colder than 35°.)

If the potatoes turn a little sweet, leave them out in your kitchen at normal temperatures for about one week, and their original flavor should be restored.

❋ Spade vegetable garden and add organic matter which will break down by next spring. (If you mulched carrots and other root crops in October, you can continue to harvest.)

INTERIOR PLANTS

❋ Purchase bulbs for forcing and indoor winter blooming. (See page 65.)

❋ For continuous blooming of forced bulbs throughout the winter, only "graduate" one or two pots per week from a 40° location to a 50° location. The bulbs can remain in the 40° location for several months.

❋ In mid-November, pot bulbs for holiday blooming. (See box this page.)

❋ Bring out amaryllis to begin forcing bloom.

GENERAL

❋ Create and build a rock garden. (See the list on page 146.)

❋ Turn the compost pile. (See How-To Tip on page 111.)

NOVEMBER
MAINTENANCE TIPS

Some bulbs, like paperwhites and amaryllis, do not have to be placed in the cold for 13 to 15 weeks before they will bloom. Simply pot the bulbs and care for as you would any houseplant. Paperwhites will bloom about five weeks after planting; amaryllis in about eight weeks.

WINTER

December, January

DECEMBER
MAINTENANCE TIPS

....

....

....

....

....

....

There are several basic rules when adding lighting to your home landscape. Do not put in "runway" lighting (a term for lining your driveway or sidewalk with lights) because all you create is a focus on the lights themselves, not aspects of the landscape. Remember the areas that are left dark are as important as those you light – contrast is visually appealing. Start with lighting in or around trees. You can hide the lighting source and at the same time move the lighting away from the house for more visual appeal. Put lights on the ground shining up, under trees, or create "moon" lighting by hiding the light fixtures up in your trees.

PERENNIALS/ ANNUALS/ BULBS

❊ Check stored bulbs to make sure they aren't sprouting or rotting. (See page 59.)

❊ Spread evergreen branches throughout the garden beds and in pots to give a festive feel to the landscape and to provide extra protection for plants.

TREES AND SHRUBS

❊ A miniature tree (bonsai) in a nice pot makes a unique and appreciated gift any time of the year! (If the receiver will keep the bonsai indoors rather than plant it outside, check with your local garden center. Only certain trees, shrubs, and vines can be kept indoors full time as bonsai.)

❊ Add lighting to your landscape.

❊ Plant your live Christmas tree in the hole dug in November.

* In higher elevations, live Christmas trees should not be left inside for more than five days or the tree may start to put on new growth. The shock will be too great after the tree is moved outside and it could die.

ROSES

* In higher elevations or for tender rose bushes, if you haven't mounded your rose bushes with 8"+ of mulch, it still isn't too late. (See How-To Tip on page 115.)

INTERIOR PLANTS

* Place your poinsettia where it will receive as much indoor light as possible. Keep it moist, and don't allow it to dry out.

How should you care for a poinsettia? Here are some ideas:

Poinsettias are one of the most common holiday plant purchases. If taken care of, a poinsettia will bloom for several months and keep its leaves until summer.

Put it in a place where the nighttime temperature won't drop below a consistent 60°. Daytime temperature should remain consistent and not exceed 80°.

DECEMBER
MAINTENANCE TIPS

....

....

....

....

....

....

....

Before bringing a potted live Christmas tree into the house, keep it in a somewhat cold place (preferably a garage) for two days first. Once inside, place the tree away from heating ducts, in a cool dry spot away from direct sunlight. Put it in a container large enough to fit the root ball and cover with some type of mulch, such as wood chips. Keep the root ball moist. Plant your live Christmas tree (see How-To Tip on page 120) in the hole prepared in November. (Move the tree to the garage first for several days to harden off.) Thoroughly water the tree after planting and again each month until spring (see How-To Tip on page 124).

DECEMBER
MAINTENANCE TIPS

....

....

....

....

....

....

....

....

Keep a cut Christmas tree outside in a bucket of water until you are ready to bring it inside. Cut several inches off the bottom of the trunk and water it. The best thing you can do to help a cut tree last is to give it plenty of water, especially the first week. Another remedy to help your tree last longer is to mix a solution of one–half cup of bleach, 2 tablespoons of sugar, and one gallon of water. Pour the mixture into the tree basin, and refill as necessary. The bleach kills bacteria in the basin, and the sugar/water helps to prevent the needles from drying out. (Don't use this remedy if you have pets!)

❋ The decorative foil plant sleeves that come with plants such as poinsettias, azaleas, and Christmas cactus prevent the pot from draining easily after watering. Poke a few holes in the sleeve, or get rid of it altogether and put the plant in a nice basket or larger pot.

❋ A Christmas cactus is a great plant for the holidays.

How should you care for a Christmas cactus? Here are some ideas:

To help your Christmas cactus bloom, the plant should be kept in a sunny location, but not direct sunlight.

It also will bloom better when kept in a place where the temperatures are about 50° to 55° at night.

Keep the plant away from any kind of hot air.

A Christmas cactus doesn't need a lot of water. Don't overwater your Christmas cactus during November and December.

If you fertilize, use a low nitrogen, high phosphorus mixture (10–30–10).

* Bring potted spring bulbs into a warmer, light location (55°) for forcing at the end of this month. (See page 65.)

* Reduce watering of houseplants as the days become shorter. They can be overwatered if you are watering as much as you do in late spring, summer, and early fall.

* If you haven't started forcing an amaryllis, you can do it early this month.

GENERAL

* Fresh cut Christmas trees should not be left in the house for more than three weeks. (See page 71.)

* Give your friends a garden basket for the holidays.

What can you include in a garden gift basket? Here are some ideas:

Start with a copy of MONTH-TO-MONTH GARDENING!

Include notecards made with the photographs from MONTH-TO-MONTH GARDENING. (Call 888-GARDEN-8 to order.)

How about a metal bookmark that can later be used as a decoration in the garden?

Seed catalogs help with planning in January.

Maybe a tulip or daffodil that you've forced in a pretty pot?

DECEMBER
MAINTENANCE TIPS

Location, location, location. A bird feeder should be put where you can see the birds, but not near trees because the food will encourage squirrels. If possible, put the feeder near a protected overhang, but not so close to the windows that birds will fly into them. Birds like to eat suet, and black oil sunflower seed is popular among most species of birds. Providing water to your feathered friends is a nice bonus, but you will have to contend with ice and freezing each day. If you plan to feed the birds, be committed – for their sake!

DECEMBER
MAINTENANCE TIPS

....

....

....

....

....

....

....

Decorate with plants and blossoms from the garden during December! Grapevines, Virginia creeper, and silverlace all make beautiful runners and window trimmings. Cornstalks, ornamental corn, dried gourds, or some of the flowers from your garden that you dried in the fall will provide welcome touches. Holly berries, rose hips, and the berries from cranberry cotoneasters are beautiful as a complement to other decorations. Arrangements can be made using twigs from shrubs such as Apache plume (white branches), red twig dogwood (red branches), and Oregon grape.

A trowel and/or leather gardening gloves are always welcome additions to a gardening basket.

A gift certificate from your local garden center is inspiring.

Instead of using a basket as a container for everything, why not a big floppy straw hat?

✸ Set out food for birds that may call your garden home. (See box page 72.)

✸ If moisture is below normal, make certain to water trees, shrubs and your lawn. (See How-To Tip on page 124.)

✸ If moisture is below normal, continue to water the compost pile.

Here are some thoughts and ideas about winter composting in higher elevations:

In higher elevations, it is not warm enough for the decomposition process to take place, so composting stops during the winter months.

Composting will resume in early March, so begin watering again at that time.

Don't add any materials to the pile during winter months. The materials you've added will freeze and smell later when decomposition begins again.

To compost during winter months, consider trying a redworm composting bin inside, using kitchen waste.

PERENNIALS/ ANNUALS/ BULBS

* Check stored bulbs for signs of dryness or rotting. (See page 59.)

* Check to make sure the mulch is still covering plants that are exposed to the south and southwest.

* If you didn't get around to this in December, lay evergreen branches from Christmas trees on perennial beds, areas where bulbs are planted, and around rose bushes to help protect plants.

* Prepare to create a topiary made of flowers.

Plan and buy materials for a topiary that you can start inside, from seed, in February. Here is one idea:

Plant a combination of morning glories, four o'clocks and moonflowers in a large pot. Follow the spacing instructions. (You can do this in a smaller pot as well; just plant fewer.)

Once the plants are growing, invert a tomato cage (or any other open wire or plastic structure that the plants can be "trained" to climb) and attach it to the top of your pot.

As the plants grow, "train" them (gently guide them) to grow up the structure on top of the pot.

JANUARY
MAINTENANCE TIPS

The following companies are good choices when ordering short-season vegetable seeds: Johnny's Select Seed, 207–437–4301, www.johnnyseeds.com; High Altitude Gardens, 800–874–7333; Vesey's Seeds Ltd., 902–368–7333, www.veseys.com; The Cook's Garden, 800–457–9703, www.cooksgarden.com; W. Attee Burpee & Co., 800–888–1447; Shepherd's Garden Seeds, 860–482–3638, www.shepherdseeds.com; D.V. Burrell's, 719–254–3318; Plants of the Southwest, 800–788–7333, www.plantsofthesouthwest.com; and Lake Valley, 707–642–4167 www.midcitynursery.com.

JANUARY
MAINTENANCE TIPS

....

....

....

....

....

....

Rotating the location of where you plant your vegetables each year in your kitchen garden is important for two reasons. First, any disease that doesn't die out over the winter won't easily spread to a different family of vegetables in the next growing season. Second, different families of vegetables use different nutrients from the soil. Rotating will prevent reduction of those nutrients from the same places in the garden. Rotate: cabbage family (cabbage, brussel sprouts, turnips); solanaceae family (tomatoes, potatoes, and peppers); alliums (garlic and onions); beans and peas; and corn.

When the weather is warmer, move your topiary outside.

❋ Plan for a "Winter Garden" next season.

We have four distinctly different seasons, and each one can bring gardening enjoyment. Here are some ideas for a Winter Garden:

Only plan for what you can see, either from inside or as a focal point in front of your home.

A Winter Garden needs a lot of structure. Incorporate not only plants, but rocks, stone, water features, and garden art.

Evergreen shrubs form a nice basis for the garden. Arrange several specialty conifers together. They come in different sizes, shapes, textures, and hues of green and blue.

After establishing structure, fill in the landscape with ornamental grasses, shrub roses, or plants that have colorful branches. (See the list on page 144.)

A Winter Garden is especially spectacular when it is lighted. (See page 69.)

TREES AND SHRUBS

❋ Gently brush the snow off trees and shrubs if you live in higher elevations.

❋ Apply dormant oil spray when temperature is above 32°.

ROSES

✻ Review catalogs for purchasing roses from mail order sources or your local garden center.

KITCHEN GARDEN

✻ Review seed catalogs for short season or new and exciting vegetable varieties. (See page 74.)

✻ Plan an herb garden or window box.

There are some considerations when planning a container herb garden. Here are some ideas:

Order the seeds now; sow the seeds indoors in February.

Move the containers outdoors when the weather permits. (Herb gardens can be grown indoors, but they are easier to tend, and less trouble outdoors.)

Container herb gardens can be grown in almost any space where you can put the container! They are suitable for people who have trouble getting around a larger garden. They can be planted on balconies, rooftops, and in window boxes.

JANUARY
MAINTENANCE TIPS

To really clean the leaves of houseplants, mix a solution of 1 ounce of vegetable oil and 23 ounces of water and mix well. Spray the leaves of the plants. It's not necessary to wipe them afterward, but if you do, support each leaf underneath with your hand and wipe carefully with terrycloth. You can also wear an old sock like a mitt and wipe down the plants. Caution: Some houseplants, such as those with hairy leaves, may not like this treatment. Try one or two leaves first before using on the entire plant.

JANUARY
MAINTENANCE TIPS

....

....

....

....

....

....

....

It's important that you fertilize interior plants with only a slow–release fertilizer because it will not really take effect until the plants need it – beginning in late March or April. Slightly reduce the amount of water you are giving houseplants now because daylight hours are minimal and plants need less water now. Overwatering can lead to problems like fungus gnat infestations.

If you're going to eventually harvest the herbs, it's practical to plant one variety per container. If you want mostly "show," then plant a variety of herbs in one large container.

Don't overfill the pot. Follow the spacing instructions on the package.

As with any garden, don't plant shade–loving herbs together with sun–loving herbs. One of them will suffer if you do!

Your container should have holes in the sides (preferable), or bottom, for proper drainage.

If you use good potting soil, found at your local garden center, you don't need to put rocks in the bottom of the container.

Follow the watering instructions as given for interior plants on this page.

✳ Plan to rotate your kitchen garden vegetables every two years. (See page 75.)

INTERIOR PLANTS

✳ Clean the leaves of all houseplants. (See box page 76.)

✳ Fertilize all houseplants with a slow-release fertilizer. (See box this page.)

GENERAL

✳ Use kitty-litter, sand, or bird-seed on icy paths and driveways. Do not use salt or chemicals that can build up in the soil and eventually cause problems for plants.

✳ Leave the compost pile alone.

✳ If moisture is less than normal, you will need to water your trees, shrubs, lawn, and possibly roses. (See How-To Tip on page 124.)

Winter watering is important. Here are some ideas:

Check the ground several inches down and, if it's dry, then water. (Overwatering isn't good for the plants either!)

Don't let the water form puddles on the surface, especially if it could freeze and turn to ice.

Water midday (between 10 a.m. and 2 p.m.) when daytime temperatures are near 50°, and the ground is not frozen (or in higher elevations, covered with snow).

JANUARY
MAINTENANCE TIPS

If you own a water feature, the frequency and amount that you seed it with a dry bacteria is determined by the type of system that you own and the time of year. Seed at least twice a year. Purchase the dry bacteria from a hardware store or garden center. With a clean coffee can or small bucket, scoop some water out of the feature and add the bacteria to the water per directions on the product. Stir and let stand for a few minutes and then pour the mixture back into your water feature. Bacteria is a vital part of your water feature because it helps to keep your water clean and establish your ecosystem.

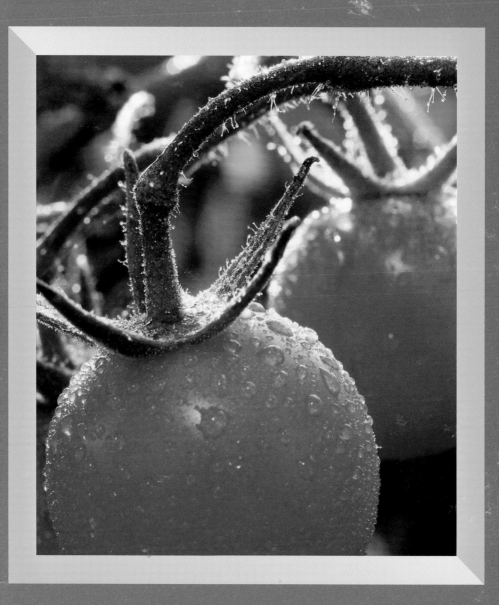

DESIGNS

PATIO GARDEN

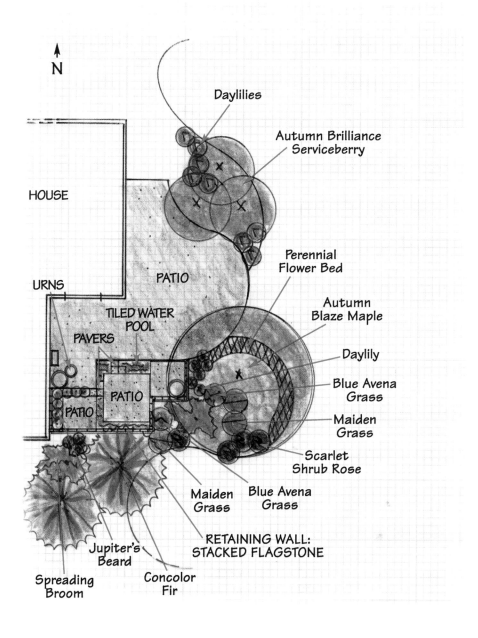

N

Daylilies

Autumn Brilliance
Serviceberry

HOUSE

PATIO

Perennial
Flower Bed

URNS

Autumn
Blaze Maple

TILED WATER
POOL

PAVERS

Daylily

PATIO

Blue Avena
Grass

PATIO

Maiden
Grass

Scarlet
Shrub Rose

Maiden   Blue Avena
Grass   Grass

RETAINING WALL:
STACKED FLAGSTONE

Jupiter's
Beard

Concolor
Fir

Spreading
Broom

 Patio Garden

A patio garden is a commentary on what makes life here so appealing. For at least six months of the year, you will find no better outdoor living. Even in the winter, many days are touched with our warm sun, so you can relax on your patio and enjoy the fresh air, the birds, and the sunshine.

Benefits: A well-designed and well-constructed patio garden creates an extension of your home that serves to carry your interior ambiance outside and the exterior environment inside. Patio gardens can express your lifestyle. You may prefer a private, intimate setting or you may use your patio for entertaining and socializing. Maybe your patio is one of your children's play areas. Creatively designed, some patios can function as all three. The plantings in your patio garden will be enjoyed in close proximity as you sit and relax, so you should plant some of your favorites. Plant material that is considered less hardy, such as redbuds, Japanese maples, and the tender perennials, can be successfully grown around the patio because of protection from the house and possibly enclosure walls.

Space and Size: Patios and their gardens come in all shapes and sizes, yet all are formed by available space and the primary functions needed to accommodate your lifestyle. Consider the use of the space. A rule of thumb is that a 12' diameter patio should be the minimum for a 4' round table with chairs. In general, consider what you want to be able to do on your patio and start with the functional requirements of the space.

Siting: Most patio gardens are located at the rear of the residence. This allows the barbecue location to be near the kitchen, and also maintains the concept of bringing the outdoors into the residence. Sometimes patio gardens can be located away from the house and in the landscape as a destination seating area.

Materials: The materials chosen will determine the ambiance created and the construction cost. Materials chosen for freestanding and retaining walls should harmonize with the house. A brick Tudor house shouldn't have timber retaining walls — matching brick or red flagstone would be better. Paving materials range in cost, with gray concrete the least expensive to mortared buff flagstone as one of the most expensive paving options. Aesthetic considerations are that drylaid brick pavers, stone, and wood decks are more casual, and conversely, mortared brick and stone are more formal. If your budget requires a less than "top of the line" paving material, you can upgrade the look of the patio with an outstanding surrounding garden.

Mortared brick and stone paving set onto a concrete subbase provides a solid and long-lasting patio. However, drylaid patios of brick or cut stone are very durable and sometimes better in areas of expansive soils. The brick or stone can easily be reset if heaving or settling problems occur. Drylaid patios also are less expensive than the mortared application.

Other considerations for your patio are lighting and shade. Patios are used most often in the afternoon and evening. Shade in the late afternoon and soft lighting will extend the enjoyment of your garden into the late evening hours.

Soil and Soil Amendments: Amend the existing soil around your patio for the garden as you would for any other garden. (See page 127.) You may want to "double-dig" the areas where you are proposing annuals and perennials. However, the key is to improve your existing soil, not totally replace it, no matter how small the garden is.

Insects and Diseases: These will be the same as you find on page 129, with some additional considerations. The microclimates created by some patio gardens will cause certain areas to be more susceptible to mites. If you are afraid of bees, avoid plants that bloom when few other plants are blooming. Succulent ground covers and ornamental grasses attract few bees. If you like to watch butterflies, grow plants that attract them. (See page 39.)

Watering: If you can manage it, drip irrigation is the most effective and efficient watering solution for patio gardens. Pop-up irrigation also should be considered, but the small planting spaces around some patios need to be carefully designed to avoid overspray. The key is not to overwater since this could put additional stress on the patio structure as well as the plants.

A Special Note: When selecting the plant materials for your patio space, the overriding factor is that you will be in close proximity to the plantings. Texture, color, fragrance, and size are the most important considerations. Fine-textured plants usually are better than coarse-textured plants; flowers can be subdued as well as bright. It's good to have some white flowers for night enjoyment. In most residential patio gardens, the smaller dwarf varieties of plants are the best choice.

XERISCAPE GARDEN

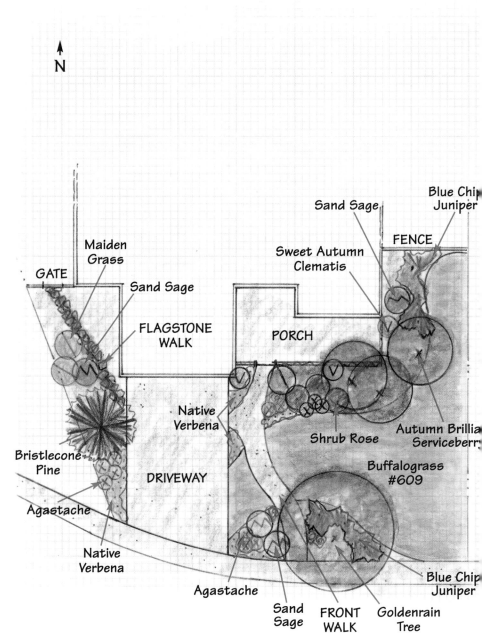

N

Blue Chip Juniper

Sand Sage

FENCE

Maiden Grass

Sweet Autumn Clematis

GATE

Sand Sage

FLAGSTONE WALK

PORCH

Native Verbena

Shrub Rose

Autumn Brillia Serviceberr

Bristlecone Pine

Buffalograss #609

Agastache

DRIVEWAY

Native Verbena

Blue Chip Juniper

Agastache

Sand Sage

FRONT WALK

Goldenrain Tree

XERISCAPE GARDEN

eriscaping means water-efficient landscaping. The root word "xeric" is Greek for dry." Because our state receives relatively little moisture, the xeric approach to ndscaping has become quite popular in recent years.

nefits: Less is more. A xeriscape garden takes less maintenance, requires less oney, and is an ecologically sound way to garden here, requiring less water, wer fertilizers, and fewer chemicals. A xeriscape garden provides a great habitat r birds and wildlife.

ructure: Take a look at what Mother Nature has done and you will find the basic ructural components that can form your xeriscape garden. Use small amounts sod or turf; design to flow with the natural landscape; and place plants based on where they grow normally (north, south, east, west). Place shrubs in groupings, ant flowers together in designated beds, and use plants that don't need much ter. Taller shade trees conserve energy; smaller evergreen trees can be effective reens and look good year-round.

ils and Soil Amendments: For buffalograss, work the soil down about 6", no amending eded. If you have to use Kentucky bluegrass or tall fescue, work the soil down out 6", amending with compost or sphagnum peat. In flower beds, rototill and work e soil down about 10" to 12" and amend the soil with a compost and peat moss ix. Shrubs can be planted to the size of the ball or container, no amending needed.

sects and Diseases: For powdery mildew, cut back the foliage on the plants when ey are done blooming, and remove all fallen leaves.

Special Note: Don't cover your landscape with Kentucky bluegrass! Instead, think out using buffalograss, at least in the backyard areas. Buffalograss uses about 60% ss water than Kentucky bluegrass (which requires 24" of water per year), it looks od with minimal watering, and it requires about three-fourths less mowing.

KITCHEN GARDEN

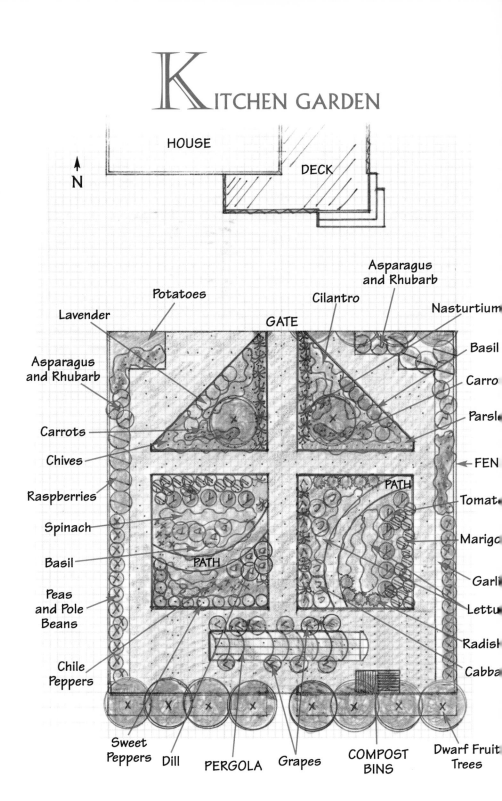

N

HOUSE

DECK

Asparagus and Rhubarb

Lavender

Potatoes

Cilantro

GATE

Nasturtium

Basil

Asparagus and Rhubarb

Carro

Carrots

Parsl

Chives

FEN

Raspberries

PATH

Tomat

Spinach

Marigo

Basil

PATH

Peas and Pole Beans

Garl

Lettu

Chile Peppers

Radish

Cabba

Sweet Peppers

Dill

PERGOLA

Grapes

COMPOST BINS

Dwarf Fruit Trees

KITCHEN GARDEN

kitchen garden is a feel-good garden. It's rewarding to put little transplants in the ound, care for them, watch them grow, and finally produce something you can tually eat (or give to your friends to eat). Believe it or not, a garden of vegetables d herbs is one of the easiest to grow.

ructure: Find a level area in your yard, preferably near the house so it's easier to nd and close to a water source. (Plus, you can watch your garden grow!) You ant the garden to get full sun for at least eight hours each day during the ring and summer months.

ed catalogs are a good way to find vegetables and herbs that you might like to ow. Then go to your garden center and buy transplants, unless you have the time start your plants from seed indoors. If the garden center doesn't carry what you ant, ask questions. It may be that your choice for a plant doesn't grow well here.

sic, or "hot" season vegetables, like warmer summer temperatures and are ready ter the first frost. "Cool" season vegetables grow best in the cooler temperatures mmon in the early spring and late fall. After two or three seasons of gardening, u will understand the vegetables and herbs you like to grow well enough to plant ccession crops.

thways provide space for walking, weeding, and harvesting. A good mulch would be to 3" of seed-free straw on the top of newspaper. You can sprinkle grass clippings er this during the growing season to add nitrogen to the soil and help control weeds. n't use grass clippings from a chemically treated lawn. You also can mulch with od chips, but use these sparingly because they change soil chemistry over time.

atering: Water your garden daily during the hottest days of the summer and every her day during the cooler months. Plants like direct watering, especially in the ottest, driest months of summer. You also can give plants different amounts of ater. For example, corn and cucumbers like lots of water, while herbs do better with ss. The best time to water is early in the morning, before 10 a.m. This also helps nserve water.

Special Note: Plant flowers in and among your vegetables and herbs, lining the erimeter and pathways of your kitchen garden. Some plants, like nasturtiums and ll, are not only edible, but serve as great insect disrupters. In addition, the flowers n be spiritually and aesthetically pleasing to the senses.

WHIMSICAL GARDEN

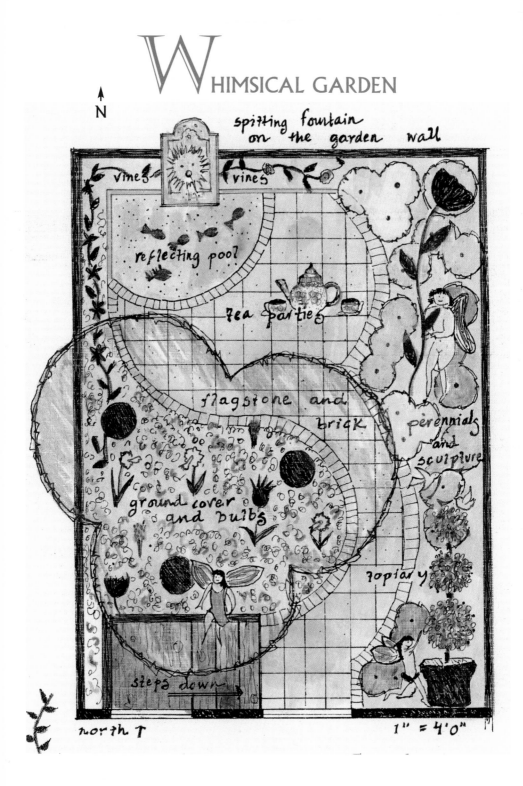

N

spitting fountain
on the garden wall

vines   vines

reflecting pool

tea parties

flagstone and
brick

perennials
and
sculpture

ground cover
and bulbs

topiary

steps down

north ↑

1" = 4'0"

WHIMSICAL GARDEN

The whimsical garden reflects a spirit of fun and creativity. Each whimsical garden is unique, reflecting the spirit of its owner and maker. Underlying every whimsical garden is practical garden design, construction, and maintenance.

Start your whimsical garden with a strong site plan. Consider scale (Is this a patio home or a ranch?), grading (Does water pool anywhere? Do you need to retain slopes?), orientation (What is the sun/shade exposure of the high-use areas?), and use (Do you play touch football regularly or raise prize-winning roses?). Think your site plan through carefully. Getting the basic, big ticket items in the right place and at the right size the first time around makes you happy, setting the stage for whimsy.

Set the whimsical garden character by selecting high-quality construction materials and building things right. If the building skills available to you are limited, choose a simple design. A well-executed, simple design will enhance the whimsy in your garden. Artful details don't cover up poor-quality construction. Always do the best you can on basics.

"Grow" your whimsy by planting for your site. Don't try to grow English ivy in full sun or sun flowers in the shade. Sick plants aren't whimsical. Maximize your growing success with irrigation — options include drip, micro-spray, and laser drip technology. Update your clock for state-of-the-art irrigation programming. Use interesting foliage (variegated euonymus) or an interesting form (globe spruces) to enliven a potentially deadly foundation planting. Pop in a crazy plant, like a spiraled juniper, a Red Hot Poker, or a globe thistle for genuine Dr. Seuss® whimsy. Don't forget to smell the roses, the lilacs, and the Carlesii viburnum.

Details, details, details. Art and ornament don't make a whimsical garden, but you can't make a whimsical garden without them. Garden centers are awash in nifty decorative items. Buy some. Little things aren't always the most whimsical. Use sculpture boldly. Art doesn't lose its leaves in the winter.

Light it up. Night lighting can accent a special artwork or lead you along a favorite path. Varying the lighting locations (from above or below), brightness, and fixtures creates nighttime magic while keeping your house and garden safer.

Finally, trust yourself. This is your garden. Go for it. If your garden isn't fun, why bother?

Water Garden

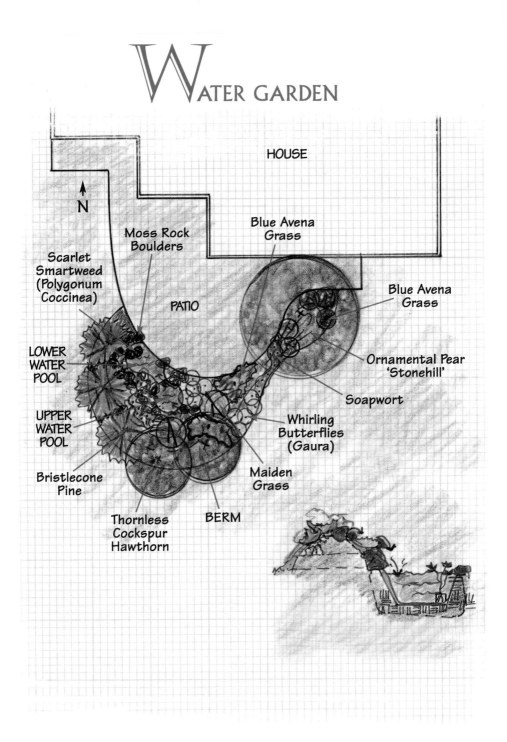

HOUSE

N

Blue Avena
Grass

Moss Rock
Boulders

Scarlet
Smartweed
(Polygonum
Coccinea)

PATIO

Blue Avena
Grass

LOWER
WATER
POOL

Ornamental Pear
'Stonehill'

Soapwort

UPPER
WATER
POOL

Whirling
Butterflies
(Gaura)

Bristlecone
Pine

Maiden
Grass

Thornless
Cockspur
Hawthorn

BERM

WATER GARDEN

A water garden is a way to create your own private Eden. It creates a peaceful setting, and the calming sound of water helps you focus your attention on what is pleasant and peaceful rather than on the traffic or airplanes or the other unpleasant noises in your environment.

Structure: Location is very important. A natural gentle slope is perfect, but soil also can be built up into berms to accommodate upper pools and waterfalls. Place the water garden in a location where it can be seen from inside the house so it can be enjoyed in all seasons.

There are generally two types of water features. With those that are more formal, you will see a lot of concrete and quarried rocks. More often, you will see informal water features that appear to be a natural part of the environment. Pea gravel and river cobble can be used to create a more natural look inside and along the borders of the pond. Grade, and then place boulders around the water feature so that natural runoff will not flow into the pond. Mud, lawn fertilizers, and insecticides can contaminate the water and kill fish and plants.

The site should receive at least five or six hours of sunlight for best success with water plants and surrounding plantings. Keep year-round interest, variation of texture and shape, and succession of color in mind when choosing plants. Character pines and dwarf spruce make lovely additions to water gardens. Avoid planting large and messy shrubs or trees adjacent to the edge of the pond, because they will drop excessive debris in the water.

Common gold fish and Koi are the types of fish used for water gardens. Don't add fish until the pool water has "cured" for a month. Fish should not be fed when the water temperature is below 50°. A small stock tank heater can be used in the winter to keep a section of the pond's surface unfrozen so fish will not suffocate.

The lowest pond should always be the largest and capable of holding the contents of the upper ponds and stream without overflowing when the waterfall is not in operation. A good size for the lower pond is about 10' by 15'. The minimum depth of a pond should be around 2½' to 3' to successfully overwinter fish. Shelves or planting pockets can be created at the sides of the pond to hold water plants needing 18" in depth.

Water features should be allowed to run even in winter. Ice forming on waterfalls and fountains is particularly interesting. Make sure the waterline below the ice is sufficient for pump operation.

CONTAINER GARDEN

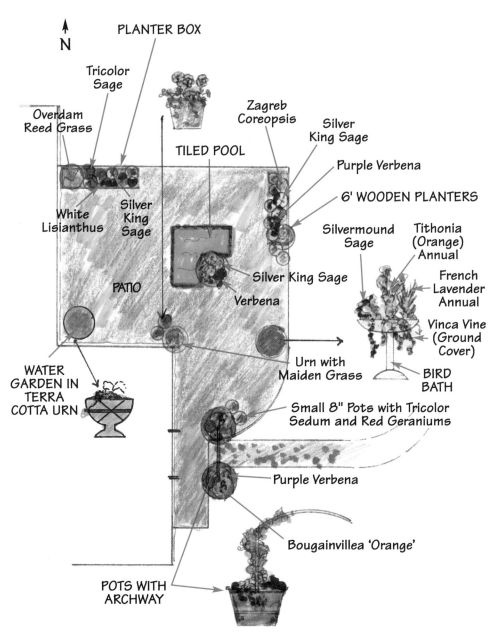

N

PLANTER BOX

Tricolor Sage

Overdam Reed Grass

Zagreb Coreopsis

Silver King Sage

Purple Verbena

TILED POOL

6' WOODEN PLANTERS

White Lisianthus

Silver King Sage

Silvermound Sage

Tithonia (Orange) Annual

French Lavender Annual

PATIO

Silver King Sage

Verbena

Vinca Vine (Ground Cover)

WATER GARDEN IN TERRA COTTA URN

Urn with Maiden Grass

BIRD BATH

Small 8" Pots with Tricolor Sedum and Red Geraniums

Purple Verbena

Bougainvillea 'Orange'

POTS WITH ARCHWAY

CONTAINER GARDEN

Your container garden should be an experience: to create, to plant, to nurture, and to enjoy. You can try things that you would never attempt in your garden beds. Be adventuresome! Or whimsical! Or fanciful! If something isn't working, just do a little rearranging and you have a new look.

The container garden shown here has several unique elements. You might try just one of them as a focal point and then plant surrounding containers based on your available time and energy level.

The 14" terra cotta urn to the far left contains a water garden. Line it with 32ml PVC, and glue it to the urn. Set a small bubbler fountain and pump inside, and add a water plant, like a water lily.

The pathway leading to the garden at the bottom of the design features two Italian terra cotta pots that support a copper archway between them. Planted in each pot are bougainvillea vines that will grow up the copper tubing, forming an arbor.

The bird bath to the right of the design is made of stained concrete and planted with herbs and vines.

The in-ground pool in the upper middle area of the patio is shallow, only 8" deep. It is lined with vivid blue glazed tiles that are frost resistant.

Above the pool, to the left, is a 6' redwood planter box. It features a rock garden, complete with interesting rocks from a nearby quarry, and is planted with portulaca moss roses, ornamental grass, and herbs.

WILDLIFE GARDEN

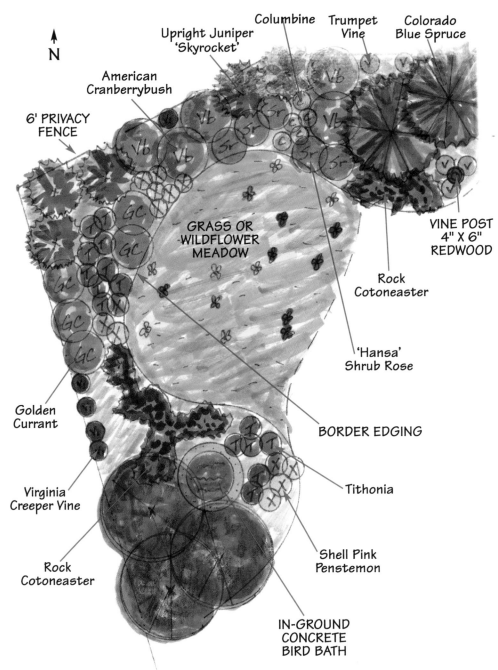

N

Columbine

Trumpet Vine

Colorado Blue Spruce

Upright Juniper 'Skyrocket'

American Cranberrybush

6' PRIVACY FENCE

GRASS OR WILDFLOWER MEADOW

VINE POST 4" X 6" REDWOOD

Rock Cotoneaster

'Hansa' Shrub Rose

Golden Currant

BORDER EDGING

Virginia Creeper Vine

Tithonia

Rock Cotoneaster

Shell Pink Penstemon

IN-GROUND CONCRETE BIRD BATH

WILDLIFE GARDEN

A wildlife garden is a backyard habitat. Designed and planted correctly, you can sit outside in your own private wildlife sanctuary and feel that you are miles from home, with only the birds, bees, and butterflies for company.

Structure: Wildlife gardens can be created from any existing location, such as a suburban backyard. The goal is to create an environment that will provide food, water, and shelter for birds, butterflies, and bees.

The best design is what nature provides. If you copy Mother Nature, it's more ecologically sound and will attract the wildlife. Create shelter with shrubs that have sweeping branches. Shrubs, trees, and perennials also provide different heights. Layers are necessary to meet the varied needs of the wildlife. (A wren has different requirements than a robin, for instance.) Screening provided by taller trees in the background provides a wind buffer for butterflies.

Plants that offer plenty of branches and nesting materials are important. Food sources can be berries, seeds, nectar, and pollen from flowers, shrubs, grasses, and trees. (Butterflies and bees need particular types of flowers to land on for their food. The way their mouths are shaped, nectar and pollen are the food sources for butterflies and bees.) Introduce water, which is essential in attracting wildlife.

Insects and Diseases: It's important when designing and creating a wildlife garden to look toward the native plants in your area. If you use native plant materials, you will have fewer problems with diseases, and pests will be controlled through natural predators attracted by the wildlife.

Special Note: More adventurous gardeners might consider including bats and reptiles in their plans. Consider adding a bat house to your garden. A bat can eat 500 insects a night. Turtles, lizards, snakes, frogs, and salamanders also prey on insects and on rodents. They will be attracted to pools and ponds.

WINDOWBOX HERB GARDEN

Winter
Savory

Sweet
Lavender

Purple
Sage

French
Lavender
Annual

'Mammoth'
Basil

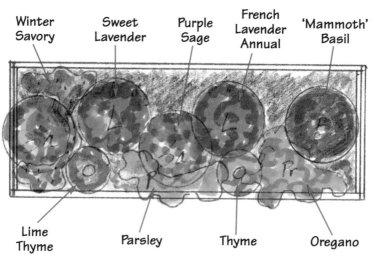

Lime
Thyme

Parsley

Thyme

Oregano

Tricolor
Sage

Sweet
Lavender

Parsley

Purple
Sage

French
Lavender
Annual

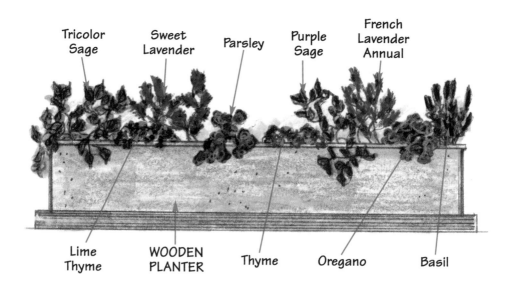

Lime
Thyme

WOODEN
PLANTER

Thyme

Oregano

Basil

WINDOWBOX HERB GARDEN

What could be better? Your windowbox not only looks beautiful, but produces plants that are good to eat! And because you're providing an almost perfect environment for growth, you have a garden that takes very little work.

Benefits: A windowbox provides good drainage, which herbs need. It also gets the plants up into the sunlight, which herbs also need. It keeps bees (herbs attract bees) away from the walkways, and you'll have fewer weeds, pests, and diseases.

Structure: A windowbox herb garden can actually be planted in any kind of container as long as it is in the sun. (Most herbs need at least some sun to grow.) The container should be 12" to 18" deep, with good drainage.

You can design and grow your herb garden based on a theme. Grow a windowbox of herbs that are good for making salsa. Or grow herbs for Italian cooking. A garden with herbs for grilling can be especially pretty as well as tasty. Of course, you can grow a mix of all kinds of herbs.

Make sure the tallest plants are in back so they don't block the sun from the shorter plants. Sages will get quite large after the first year and will require pruning.

Soil and Soil Amendments: Buy a professional potting mix for containers at your garden center.

Fertilizer: You will need to fertilize periodically. Add a small amount of compost to the windowbox once or twice each growing season. Do not over-fertilize.

Watering: The easiest way is to hand water at the base of the plants.

Border flower garden

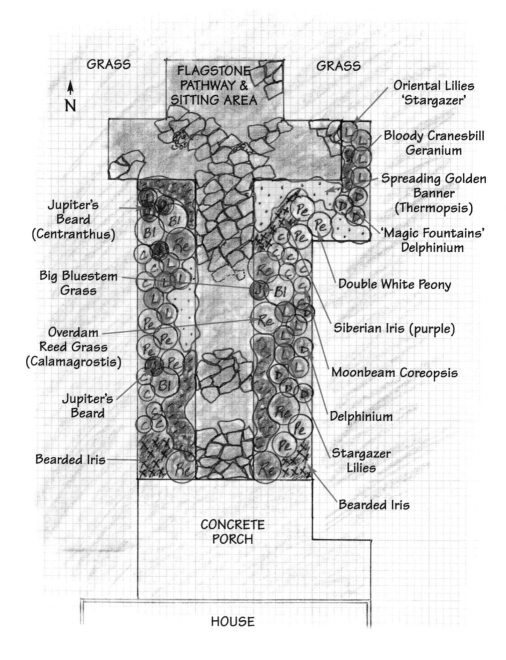

GRASS

FLAGSTONE PATHWAY & SITTING AREA

GRASS

N

Oriental Lilies 'Stargazer'

Bloody Cranesbill Geranium

Spreading Golden Banner (Thermopsis)

Jupiter's Beard (Centranthus)

'Magic Fountains' Delphinium

Big Bluestem Grass

Double White Peony

Siberian Iris (purple)

Overdam Reed Grass (Calamagrostis)

Moonbeam Coreopsis

Jupiter's Beard

Delphinium

Bearded Iris

Stargazer Lilies

Bearded Iris

CONCRETE PORCH

HOUSE

BORDER FLOWER GARDEN

Perennials and annuals dance together in a border flower garden to delight the senses like nothing else quite can. Perennials create the backbone of your garden. They can be sophisticated or simple, orderly or boisterous, flashy or subdued. Annuals dart here and there, brilliant in their colors, showing off for their one season of life.

Structure: You could plant only annuals, but what an investment of time and money every single year! Your perennials are those faithful friends who will, with a minimal amount of maintenance, show up in your garden beds beginning each March and as late as November in some microclimates. Annuals, on the other hand, give you the chance to experiment and add variety each year.

A border flower garden is generally viewed from one side. Don't place tall plants in front of the shorter ones because they obscure the view of the smaller plants. This garden can be designed formally or informally. Informal tends to have more random heights, an asymmetrical design, and grouped plants. In a formal garden, the flowers are systematically balanced and are usually planted in rows with a more precise gradation in height.

The key is to match both perennials and annuals to your particular microclimate. Choose those that work with your existing landscape. Keep in mind that the lighting here is different than in other parts of the United States. Because of the bright sunlight, we need brighter plant colors — the softer colors can appear washed out here. Start by choosing plants for their variety in foliage color and texture, then consider bloom color. This will provide a display that is attractive even when plants are between blooms.

Vary the theme. Have an all-white border flower garden. Or plant a moonlight garden using flowers that are highlighted under the moon. Try a fragrant garden, choosing plants that are the same height as in the design, but substitute with flowers that have fragrance. The garden pictured here features perennials, but you can add your favorite annuals to compliment this design.

Insects and Diseases: Maintaining a balance between insect pests and beneficial insects in the garden is important. Simple treatments, like those seen on page 129, usually will suffice to take care of flower pests and diseases if the helpful insects can't do the job on their own.

A Special Note: The traditional plants that comprise an English garden are very difficult to keep healthy here. But, you can substitute plants that will bring out the essence of this type of setting. The feel of your garden comes as much from form, texture, and layout as it does from the actual flowers.

Interior Garden

Anthurium

African Violet

Azalea

Bromeliad

Orchid

Poinsettia

Sago Palm

Christmas
Cactus

INTERIOR GARDEN

Indoor container gardening is about simplicity. You can design your garden to fit any space. If a plant outgrows where you've placed it, simply put it in another location! Diseased or infested plants can be moved, treated, and returned when healthy. Best of all, you're free to experiment with colors, heights, textures — just move the containers around!

Benefits: Plants help clean the air. Did you know that one mother-in-law's tongue plant will significantly clean the air in a 10' x 10' room in 24 hours? (Actually, any 3' tall plant will work.) The other benefit to growing plants indoors is aesthetics. Plants look great. They create balance and harmony. The result is that they make you feel good.

Structure: The considerations about which to purchase are much like the considerations for outdoor gardening. How much light does the plant need? (The sun is very intense here, so don't place any plant in the direct sunlight for a number of hours.) How large will it get? What textures and colors do you like best? Is the plant fairly disease-resistant? How much maintenance does it require? Are you willing and able to give the time? These things determine the structure of your interior garden of plants.

Soils and Soil Amendments: All-purpose potting soil with a Canadian peat base is highly recommended. An all-purpose fertilizer with a 13-13-13 breakdown should work just fine. Fertilize just once, maybe twice a year — more often can be harmful (although many gardeners like to fertilize regularly with a liquid fertilizer as long as the plant is actively growing).

Watering: The biggest fallacy is that you're supposed to let interior plants dry out between waterings. Not true. Most problems with houseplants are caused by underwatering, not overwatering. (If you are overwatering, you'll know it because the plants stand in water and will give off a musty smell.) The soil for indoor plants should be damp at all times. (Some plants *do* like to dry out between waterings, so check the requirements for each plant.)

Special Note: Grow a variety of plants in your home! Try orchids near your east-facing windows, for instance (start simple with a moth orchid and work your way up). Grow herbs in a south-facing window, or put that mother-in-law's tongue in a north-facing location.

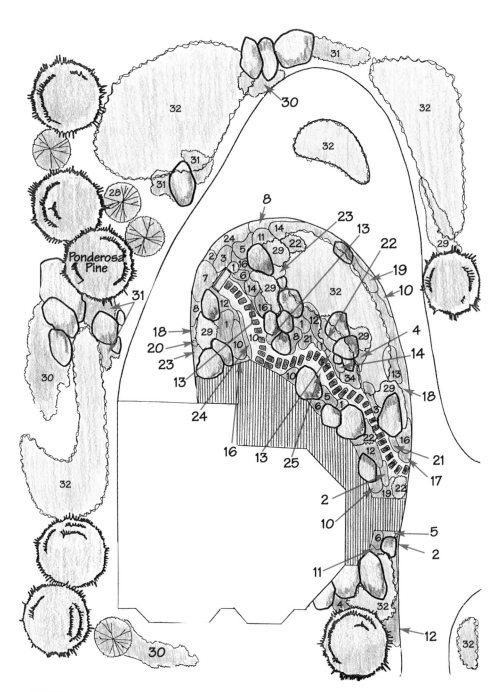

Mountain Garden

KEY:

1. False forget-me-not
2. Creeping phlox ("White Delight")
3. Peach leaf harebell, white
4. Lady's mantle
5. Fall aster ("Alert")
6. Snowdrop windflower
7. Salvia ("Mainacht")
8. Columbine (Mix - "Dove")
9. Purple coneflower
10. Geranium ("Kashmir White")
11. Columbine ("Bluejay")
12. Beardstongue
13. Cushion spurge
14. Peach leaf harebell, blue
15. Deadnettle ("Shell Pink")
16. Foxglove ("Excelsior")
    Foxglove ("Mertonensis")
    Foxglove ("Foxy")
    Foxglove ("Purpurea Alba")
17. Harebell ("White Clips")
18. Turkish Veronica
19. Beardstongue ("Rondo")
20. Harebell ("Blue Clips")
21. Geranium ("Johnson's Blue")
22. Daphne ("Rosy Glow")
23. Foxglove ("Grandiflora")
24. Creeping phlox ("Emerald Pink")
25. Vinca minor ("Bowles")
    Phlox ("Emerald Blue")
26. Creeping phlox ("Emerald Blue")
    Vinca minor ("Bowles")
    Spring bulb collection: Narcissus, grape hyacinth, crocus species tulips, dwarf iris, and snowdrops
    Columbine ("Dove" and "Bluejay")
27. Deadnettle ("Shell Pink")
    Geranium ("Johnson's Blue")
    Spring bulb collection: Narcissus, grape hyacinth, crocus species tulips, dwarf iris, and snowdrops
    Columbine ("Dove" and "Bluejay")
28. Russian hawthorn
29. Peking cotoneaster
30. Thimbleberry
31. Three leaf sumac
32. Aspen
Existing: Ponderosa pine

Mountain Garden

If you live in the mountains, you understand the need to carve out your own piece of tranquillity. In the vast expanse of the Rocky Mountains, there is comfort in defining a niche, a small, private space for yourself.

Benefits: The mountains are peaceful, quiet, and green. But even the natural beauty of the mountains and forest can be enhanced and complemented by adding colors and textures. Relief from the seasonal browns and greens that the forest bestows can be found in perennials, bulbs, and the brilliant fall reds of many selected shrubs.

Structure: Work with, not against, the existing landscape! Use the ponderosa pines to define flow; incorporate the outcroppings of moss rock into garden areas; blend your plants with the native shrubs and flowers already growing.

Garden placement needs to be planned carefully, and many items must be addressed, one of which is mountain water issues. If your area is on a well (which many are), growing your garden at the top of a steep incline may be more difficult. Large expanses of grass or plants that require a lot of water also could pose a problem if the water production is low.

Every part of the country has microclimates. Nowhere are these more apparent than in the mountains. Temperatures can fluctuate as much as 10° between one side of a landscape and another, depending on the wind, slope, grade of land, exposure, and the number of trees or amount of shade. Plant materials must be selected based on all these factors, not just plant hardiness guides.

Soil and Soil Amendments: Because of the rocks in the soil, double digging (amending the soil, then amending again see page 127) is recommended, and if possible, tilling down to a depth of 12". The good news is that if you go to this trouble in the beginning, you will only need to top dress (rake in 2" to 3" of compost) your gardens every two to three years. Good soil is absolutely imperative in mountain gardening. Unless your trees are diseased, don't rake up the pine needles because, over time, the decomposition will enrich the plants and soil.

Insects and Diseases: The major insect problems seen in the mountains are mountain pine beetle and white pine weevil, and, to a lesser extent, aphids and occasionally slugs. Both types of beetle activity need to be evaluated and addressed by professionals. Aphids and slugs are treated similarly in most areas. (See page 129.) Minimal slug problems can be treated by using a saucer of beer in the garden. Slugs are drawn to beer, fall into the liquid, and drown.

Watering: Water needs are based on the microclimates in your landscape. South side areas, or those exposed to full sun, will need more water than those on the north or in the shade. In early June and early September, it's possible to have 70° temperatures during the day and still get down to freezing at night. If your plants are well watered, they will endure better. Winter watering, preferably by hand (see page 78), is important. (Don't water on top of snow.)

A Special Note: Perennial spring and fall cleanup in the mountains is particularly important. Top dress, deadhead, cut back, prune. Your plants will be much healthier for the extra care at the beginning and at end of the growing season.

ROSE GARDEN

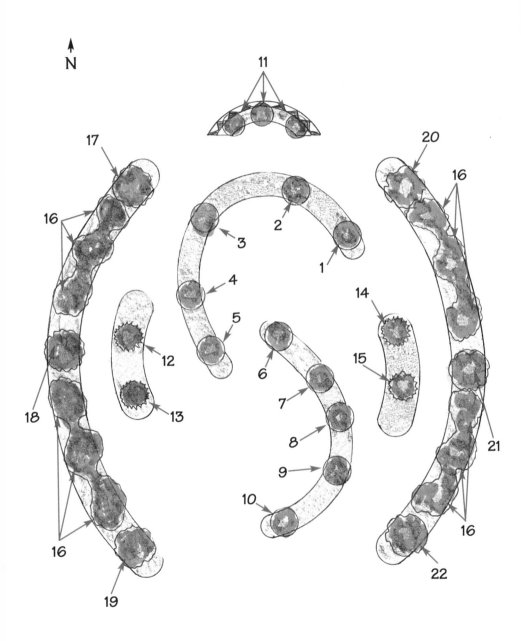

ROSE GARDEN

KEY: Hybrid Tea, Grandiflora, and Floribunda Roses (plant 3' apart)
1. Mister Lincoln (dark red)
2. Peace (yellow/shaded pink)
3. Chicago Peace (coral/shaded yellow)
4. Pascali (white)
5. Chrysler Imperial (dark red)
6. Pristine (white pink edged)
7. Queen Elizabeth (medium pink)
8. Double Delight (red/white)
9. Sutter's Gold (orange blend)
10. Garden Party

Climbing Rose (plant 2' to 3' apart)
11. America (orange pink)

Miniature Roses (plant 1½' to 2' apart)
12. Easter Morning (white)
13. Rise-n-Shine (medium yellow)
14. Stars-n-Stripes (red/white striped)
15. Starina (orange red)

Groundcover Rose (plant 3' apart)
16. White Flower Carpet

Shrub Roses (plant 5' apart)
17. Rockin Robin (red and white)
18. Linda Campbell (medium red)
19. Golden Wings (light yellow)
20. 'Coral' Meidiland
21. Sharifa Asma (light pink)
22. Rosa Rugosa Alba (white)

Rose Garden

Roses have a reputation for being one of the harder shrubs to grow. It's not true! They can be a little persnickety, they need some care, but they will grow here (and beautifully). People are discovering that there's more to roses than the hybrid teas: consider the rugosas, the old garden shrub and species roses, the damasks, the albas. (Note: the old fashioned varieties have fewer insects and disease problems.) Roses can be a tremendous contributor to the landscape during all four seasons of the year.

Benefits: Rose bushes come in all shapes, textures, colors, and sizes. They are a versatile plant, content to form the background, eager to create a focal point, or agreeable to simply exist and provide a little diversion in the landscape.

Roses can be used for things other than for show or as cut flowers. The hips, particularly, on some shrubs are magnificent. They create their own showcase in the landscape, or can be cut for use on wreaths or other arrangements. Rose petals, when dried, smell wonderful; add them to potpourri. Have you ever tried rose hip jam, rose honey, rose wine, or rose tea?

Structure: Roses do best when they are planted in locations where they get over six hours of full sun every day. They also do better when they are planted in their own beds, alone, primarily because maintenance is similar and therefore easier. There are exceptions, as you will find. Some roses, like a semi-sprawler or climber, do nicely around trees because they like both shade and sun. Speaking of climbers: Some roses are not as hardy as others. This doesn't mean you can't plant them, it just means a little more work for you. Climbing roses are an example.

When you think about which roses to plant, think about year-round color and texture. Some, like the species roses, have beautiful fall foliage. The rugosas, which also provide fall color, have tremendous hips that will last into the winter months.

A Special Note: Before you buy rose bushes, see them first! Go to your local garden center or nursery, or visit places where roses are featured to see what appeals to your senses.

HOW-TO TIPS

HOW-TO TIPS

How To Clean Indoor Container Plants

The best way to thoroughly clean indoor houseplants is to take them outdoors. The temperature must be 60° or warmer, but never place the plants in the full sun because the leaves will burn in as little as 10 minutes. To keep the soil intact and in the pots, ball up newspapers on top of the soil and put them around the base of the plant. (This also keeps bugs and dust that are cleaned off the leaves from falling in the soil.) Lay the pot on its side and spray the plant down with the garden hose. Then take a soapy water solution (1 ounce of mild dishwashing detergent like Ivory mixed with 23 ounces of water) and spray the plant thoroughly. Let the solution sit on the plant for three to five minutes, then spray it down thoroughly with the garden hose. If your plants are infested with spider mites or scale, repeat this process three weeks in a row. Let the plant dry out for several minutes in the shade and then bring it inside.

How To Compost

What is compost? It's organic matter you can use to supplement and fertilize your soil. It's full of tiny microorganisms that help provide important nutrients for your plants. It also helps break up the clay or hold moisture in sandy or rocky soil. You don't have to add compost to your soil, but your plants will grow much better if you do. The idea is to mix together things like grass clippings from lawns that have not been chemically treated, fallen leaves, pine needles, small wood chips, discarded plant materials, vegetable and fruit refuse, and coffee grounds. Let them decompose together. You then add a small amount of this decomposed material, or "compost," to the soil around your plants. There are lots of ways to make compost, but one of the easiest methods is to simply make a pile in a corner in your backyard. Keep in mind that the compost tends to attract neighborhood pets and, if not tended properly, it may smell bad. If you want to compost and you live in an urban environment, you can buy several different kinds of black plastic compost bins. There are three things you need to remember to do while composting: (1) chop up any materials going into the bin so they decompose more quickly; (2) turn the pile once a week to aid microorganisms in the decomposition process; and (3) keep the compost pile damp (not soggy!). Plant material won't decompose to form compost if the materials in the bin are too dry. Don't put animal or human waste, meat, or weeds full of seed heads in the compost bin.

How-to Tips

How To Deadhead

It's important to get rid of flower blossoms just after they have died, especially on those plants that repeat flower. Deadheading annuals and perennials leads to more blossoms, healthier plants the next year, and a better looking garden. Pinch off the individual blooms on flowers that cluster, like petunias. On flowers that grow on single leafy stems, such as daisies, cut back to just above the top growing leaves. For flowers that grow on plants such as daylilies, cut the flower back as far down as you can after it has bloomed. The stems of roses that have bloomed should be cut back at an upward slant up to where the stem is as thick as a pencil, and $1/4"$ above a leaflet. (It is generally recommended that you make your cut above a five or seven leaflet for good bloom and to allow enough strength to support the flower. Cutting back to a three leaflet often is not strong enough for good bloom.) Seal off rose stems with a dab of white household glue or commercial rose solvent.

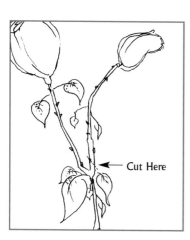

Cut Here ←

How To Keep the Deer and Elk Away

Start by growing plants that deer and elk don't like around the outside of your garden: iris, yarrow, globe thistles, sagebrush, lavender, chives, ornamental onions, garlic chives, yucca, and mountain mahogany. (Deer and elk like coneflower, peonies, hollyhocks, impatiens, crocus, daylilies, sedum, phlox, rhododendrons, roses, and tulips.) You also can structure your garden to "flow" around existing deer or elk traffic. Some people hang bars of soap from string — two or three bars to a tree. There are also deer repellents that can work, but these often need to be reapplied after every rain or snow. Of course, electric fences or specially designed elk or deer fences are the best solution.

How-To Tips

How To Deep Water

Trees and shrubs should be deep watered during every season here (unless the ground is frozen), especially during the first two years after they are planted. Roses, perennials, and lawns also should be deep watered as needed. (For minimum penetration depths for your plants and lawn, check How–To Water on page 124.) This means you need to apply water around root zones at least once a month (if the soil is not frozen), on a warm day (above 40°). Water early in the day so the water will soak in before night.

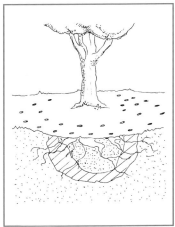

One method of deep watering trees and shrubs is to use a root feeder or a soil needle, which attaches to your garden hose. The feeder should be inserted about 8" into the soil. With new trees or shrubs, you need to water from the trunk to the "drip line" (directly below where the longest branch extends out). With more established plants, water further out, beyond the drip line. (It won't help to water near the trunk.) Holes should be approximately 1 foot apart. Angle the feeder down and away from the trunk, turn the water on to a medium level, and run in each hole for about 30 seconds.

For lawns, garden beds, roses, and landscapes with heavy clay soil, (or if you just don't want to use a deep root water needle), surface–watering is recommended. Water once a month during the winter and many times a month during the hottest summer months. Simply move the hose around the drip line of the tree or shrub for approximately 15 to 20 minutes or around various locations in your garden for 30 to 45 minutes. Watch for water pooling. This may indicate that the ground is saturated or the drainage is poor. (Most plants do not grow well in saturated, soggy soil, so reduce watering in these areas and improve soil drainage.) Don't forget to maintain 1" to 3" of mulch on your landscape all year long to conserve and retain moisture.

H OW-TO TIPS

How To Fertilize

If you amend your soil every year and water properly, most of your plants, including most perennials, annuals, bulbs, and vegetables, will not need additional fertilizer. If you think your plants need fertilizing, however, add a well–balanced organic or inorganic fertilizer. (Do not apply a balanced fertilizer in any area three years in a row.) While our soil does need more nitrogen, too much will encourage weeds and weak plant growth. Fertilizers are sold with a label that indicates the levels of nitrogen, phosphate (phosphorus), and potash (potassium). For example, a fertilizer that reads 5–10–5 on the front of the bag contains 5% nitrogen, 10% phosphorus, and 5% potassium.

You don't necessarily have to fertilize established trees and shrubs, and those that are newly planted or transplanted will benefit from only a little extra feeding. Good fertilizers are those that are slow release. This means the tree or shrub will be able to use the fertilizer as it needs it.* Feed trees through a deep feeder (see How–To Tip on page 113) or by pellet fertilizer sprinkled near the tree.

For roses, there are organic fertilizers that contain alfalfa meal, bone meal, sulfur, and iron. Roses also will thrive with a commercial fertilizer that contains equal amounts of nitrogen and potash and more phosphate. This mix helps promote root growth and blooming potential. A good mix would read 5–10–5 on the label. Sprinkle the fertilizer on top of the soil around the base of the bush, removing any mulch first, and rake it in. Then water deeply. Fertilize your rose bushes once a month during the growing season, but no later than mid–August.

Lawn grass, particularly Kentucky bluegrass, likes lots of nitrogen. When purchasing a commercial fertilizer, look for a high content of nitrogen, half as much phosphate, and then half again as much potash (20–10–5 on the label). Also make sure there is a small amount of iron in the fertilizer, and about 10% to 15% sulfur. If using an organic fertilizer, look for a slow–release fertilizer.* Buffalograss needs very little fertilizer, so one application of nitrogen in the fall should suffice.

HOW-TO TIPS

Fertilize your houseplants once a year with a time–release fertilizer that breaks down over nine months. The plant will utilize the fertilizer when it needs it most, in the late spring and summer, rather than during the winter. (Over–fertilizing houseplants can do more harm than good.) Look for a fertilizer that is labeled 13–13–13 (nitrogen, phosphate, potash). Use a soluble fertilizer when the plant is actively growing.

*Slow–release fertilizers don't work well in the mountains (except for indoor plants). Instead, use a liquid soluble or foliar feed fertilizer.

How To Mulch

Mulch is organic or inorganic matter that is placed on the ground around plants, trees, and shrubs. Mulch moderates soil temperatures, controls weeds, helps the soil retain moisture, and keeps the landscape looking neat and trim. Mulches that can be used here: gravel, wood chips, shredded bark, pine needles, and straw. Grass clippings or leaves can be used, but be sure they are disease and insect free. Old newspapers (or cardboard) also make a good mulch in vegetable and perennial gardens. Spread the newspaper around plants and everywhere that you want nothing to grow. Then cover it with a thin layer of wood chips, bark, etc. Breathable landscape fabric also works well, especially as a weed barrier, but it needs to be covered with either organic or inorganic material. Leave a few inches between the plants, trees, and shrubs and the mulch. November is a good time to mulch your perennial beds to help the soil retain badly needed moisture through the winter and to prevent the soil from heaving due to temperature fluctuations. A good time to mulch annual beds is at the time of planting, again, to help the soil retain moisture and to provide a weed barrier.

HOW-TO TIPS

How To Harvest Common Vegetables
from the Kitchen Garden

Cool–Season Vegetables

Peas: Pick when peas are 3" to 4" in length, bright green in color, and firm in texture.

Lettuce: Cut at the base of the plant near the ground when the leaves are big enough to put in salads (7" to 8" long and 4" to 5" wide, depending on the variety).

Onions: Pull them when most of the tops have fallen over. Before using, put them in a sunny, dry spot for one week.

Potatoes: Harvest potatoes when blossoms appear — usually about seven or eight weeks after they have been planted. Dig carefully around the plant and remove the larger potatoes, leaving the smaller ones so they can continue to grow. (Start digging about one foot away from the plant and "tunnel" in to minimize damage to the potato.)

Spinach: Harvest similar to lettuce or pull off outer leaves periodically for salads.

Broccoli: Cut the flowers (which are the heads) off before hot weather comes, because they will open and become bitter and inedible.

Brussel
sprouts: Pick when they are approximately 1" in diameter and green in color. Remove from the plant beginning with the sprouts at the bottom first.

Carrots: Look for shoulders (the top part of the vegetable protruding from the soil) that are 1" across and orange in color.

Main–Season or Hot–Season Vegetables

Tomatoes: Pick off plant when fruit turns a deep, rich red color. For best flavor, try to leave on the vine to ripen. When an early frost is predicted, pick green tomatoes and let ripen indoors in indirect light.

Tomatillos: Pick when the papery skin around the fruit drys out.

 How-To Tips

Radishes: Look for shoulders (the top part of the vegetable protruding from the soil) that are at least ½" across. Pull up gently. Wash off soil before storing in refrigerator. Radishes can be ready to harvest four to six weeks after planting, so watch these carefully.

Cucumbers: Pick before they grow beyond 7" in length for most varieties. Shriveled and yellow cucumbers, which taste bitter, may be due to underwatering when fruit was forming. Harvest before a hard frost.

Garlic: Pick when the tops of the plant are dry. Pull out the entire plant, braid the tops together and hang in a dry area for winter use.

Pole beans: Pick off vines before beans are full if you want to eat them entirely. If growing for seeds or "beans," let the fruit mature. Harvest before a hard frost.

Peppers: Pick off plant when the pepper is at least 3" across and fruit color is deep green (or purple, yellow, or even red lately!). Harvest before a hard frost.

Chile peppers: Pick the pod with the stem attached. (Allow for longer stems when making ristras. See page 46.) Chiles can be picked green or red. Green chile is immature and if left on the plant will turn red. If picked, green chile will shrivel and not turn a bright red color. Red chile is normally picked for winter use.

Zucchini: A type of "summer squash." Harvest when 6" long. Zucchini that gets away from you and grows bigger often tastes very bland and sometimes bitter. Harvest zucchini before a hard frost.

Herbs: The best time to pick herbs is in the morning, about 10 a.m. (You want to wait until the herbs are dry, so you don't crush them in the picking.) The leaves of herbs can be cut and used fresh at any time during the season. If you want to use the herbs later, either freeze them immediately (no moisture, in air–tight bags) or dry them out. (See page 54.) If you plan to use them later, harvest them when the plants begin to flower.

HOW-TO TIPS

How To Plant or Transplant Rose Bushes

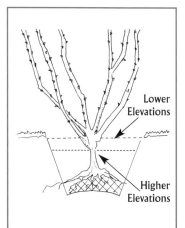

Lower Elevations

Higher Elevations

Choose a sunny site. Make sure the soil has been prepared properly (see How–To Tip on page 127), and dig a hole deep enough to plant even with the graft (or with the graft 2" below the ground in higher elevations). (The graft is a knobby area just above the roots and at the bottom of the limbs.) With bare–root or transplanted bushes, try to spread the roots out to encourage stronger root growth. Using soil, you can form a cone in the bottom of the hole to place the roots around (like a tepee). With container bushes, take the bush out of the pot and make sure to remove wires or plastic wraps before you plant. Place the bush in the hole and backfill with amended soil. You can mix in a thin layer of triple super–phosphate with soil in the bottom of the hole before planting. Soak the planted area thoroughly. Plant hybrid tea roses 2' to 2½' apart, miniature roses 1' to 1½' apart, groundcover roses 3' apart, and bush and shrub roses 4' apart.

 How-To Tips

How To Prune

There are several reasons to prune your trees and shrubs. Pruning removes dead and diseased branches, encourages a healthier plant, inspires more fruitful production, and prevents the spread of disease and insects. To a much lesser degree, careful pruning gives the tree or shrub an improved shape.

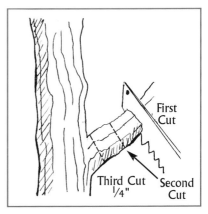

Deciduous Trees: Near the place where the trunk and the branch meet is a slight mound of bark called the collar. When you prune, cut at an angle, 1/4" outside the collar. If you cut inside the collar, the wound takes longer to heal, allowing disease and insects to get into the trunk. If you can't find a collar, make a cut at a right angle going outward from the trunk. Do not leave long stubs on the tree. Avoid cutting off main trunk limbs, but if they are diseased or already dead, prune back.

Deciduous Shrubs: If the canes are diseased or are producing weak, leggy foliage, prune the oldest and weakest canes at or near the ground. If you want trimmer, less dense plants, remove one–third of the oldest canes at the base of the plant, near the ground. Do not shear your shrubs (trimming off the top of the branches) because this causes excessive growth at the tip of the branches, which will shade out inside leaf growth. This could lead to unhealthy and diseased shrubs. Prune spring–flowering shrubs after they bloom, not in the winter.

Evergreen trees and shrubs don't need much pruning at all. In fact, keep in mind that evergreens that are cut back excessively may not grow back. If you want to control the growth of a few branches, snip the candles part way (yellow/brown growth that shoots out from the end of the branches).

How-to tips

How To Create A Miniature Orchard in Your Backyard

You can have a small orchard in your backyard, even if you have limited space. Plant two or more different fruit trees in the same hole, 18" apart. You can plant dwarf, semi-dwarf, or standard fruit trees. The benefits of close planting, besides saving space, are that the trees won't grow as big because they are competing (good pruning is a must!), and there is better cross-pollination with some varieties. The trees will still produce a nice amount of fruit, plus you almost get the impression that you are picking several kinds of fruit from one tree!

How To Plant and Transplant Trees and Shrubs

For bare-root trees and shrubs, dig the hole wide enough to spread the roots out (they shouldn't curve up the sides of the hole), and deep enough that the place where the roots and the trunk meet will be at the same level it was when growing in the nursery. (In lower elevations, usually even with the ground; in higher elevations, 2" to 3" above the ground so the soil can settle). Take two-thirds of the soil from the hole and mix it (amend) with one-third organic matter such as compost or peat moss. Shovel the amended soil around the tree until it is filled to the top of the hole. (Do not pack the soil down.) Create a mound of dirt around the outside edge of the hole, fill it with water, and let the water soak into the ground. Then water as needed. (see How-To Tip on page 124) Put 2" to 3" of mulch (see How-To Tip on page 115) around the plant.

For balled and burlapped trees and shrubs, dig the hole twice as wide as the ball and deep enough that the ball will be at the same level it was growing in the nursery. (In lower elevations, plant even with ground; in higher elevations, 2" to 3" above the ground so the soil can settle.) Take two-thirds of the soil from the hole and mix it (amend) with one-third organic matter such as compost or peat moss. It is very important to remove the wire or twine from the ball before it is planted and also remove the top third of the wire basket after the plant is placed in the hole.

HOW-TO TIPS

Cut the burlap back slightly from the tree or shrub and tuck it down around the root so it does not act like a wick (remove synthetic wrap – it will not decompose). Remove all twine from around the trunk and on top of the ball. If the ball is wrapped with shrink–wrap, remove it. Shovel the amended soil around the tree until it is filled to the top of the hole. (Do not pack the soil down.) Create a mound of dirt around the edge of the hole, fill it with water, and let the water soak into the ground. Then water as needed. (See How–To Tip on page 124.) Put

5" of mulch (see How–To Tip on page 115) around the plant.

For container trees and shrubs, follow the same directions above for balled and burlapped plants, except do the following: Take the plant out of the container carefully (make sure the soil is damp, not dry, to make this easier). If the roots appear matted around the sides, or if they circle the bottom, try to loosen and pull them away from the sides of the root ball. (Don't do this with pines.) On pines, or if you can't pull the roots away by hand, cut down the sides $1/2$" in three to four places with a knife or gardening spade. If the

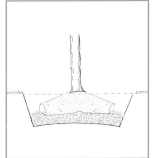

roots are all down at the bottom of the ball, take an axe, shovel, or sharp knife and, from the middle of the bottom, cut a little less than halfway up the middle of the root ball. Spread each half out to each side forming a "butterfly." (The plant actually will grow better by loosening or cutting the roots.) Place the butterflied plant on a small mound of soil in the bottom of the hole.

When transplanting, you have to make sure you dig enough of the root system to allow the tree or shrub to reestablish itself quickly in the new location. The American Nurseryman Standards chart suggests how big the root ball should be dug for the type of tree or shrub you want to transplant. Then follow the directions for planting balled and burlapped trees and shrubs. Transplanting trees and shrubs here in the fall or the middle of summer is risky.

How-to Tips

How To Stake Trees

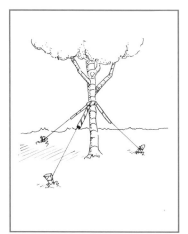

Some newly planted trees should be staked so they can establish roots. There are several pieces of hardware you must have to stake plants. The stake itself should be at least 2" wide and long enough to go down at least as deep as the bottom of the ball. The stake often is made of metal for durability. The cable that attaches the tree to the stake is called a guy wire. The wire should be attached to tree straps (made with grommets), which wrap around the trunk. Two or three stakes per tree should be enough. Don't stake the tree so tightly that the trunk can't move slightly. A little trunk movement is necessary to stimulate root growth. Make sure the bark is not being rubbed or damaged. Stake the tree only temporarily. If you have a tree that tends to tip over (spruces have a limited root system so they are especially susceptible to snow, wind, overwatering, and underwatering), then continue to stake, but move the tree straps around every few months so they are not on the same place on the trunk. Immediately after you stake, do any necessary pruning (the top one–third of the branches on bare–root trees, but do not trim the "leader" or branch that stands tallest). Water newly planted trees regularly for the first five weeks (check your soil for dryness; see How–To on page 124), then as required by the type of tree and the location.

How-To Tips

How To Weed

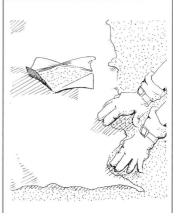

There are two types of weeds: perennial (come back every year) and annual (live one year and set seed at the end of the season). Some of the most prevalent perennial weeds in our state are thistle, bindweed, and dandelions. Annual weeds include spurge, crabgrass, punctervine, purslane, knotweed, and common chickweed. You can use weed barrier cloth to help keep weeds to a minimum in large areas. After putting the cloth down, cover with a mulch like wood chips or straw. For planting, cut holes in the cloth that are a little wider than the plant. If you use this weeding technique, remember that seeds will have to be planted only in the areas where you cut holes. In smaller areas, you can use several layers of newspaper to achieve the same thing as weed barrier cloth. If you dig or rototill the area first, try not to do it when weeds are just getting ready to reseed (after they bloom), make sure to get the weed roots, and mulch immediately. Remove the seedheads – do not till them into the soil! If weeding by hand (for weeds that are growing in and around established plants), either pull them when the soil is damp (to get the entire root) or cut them off at the base with pruners every couple of days until the weed no longer grows. Finally, you can spray weeds with a product that contains the chemical glyphosate (it breaks down in the soil). Be careful with glyphosate: it will kill any plant it contacts. In all cases, weed once a week to keep things under control and spread mulch liberally (see How–To Tip on page 115).

H OW-TO TIPS

How To Water

The climate in our state is highly varied, ranging from mountainous to semi–arid to arid. Overall, however, we don't get a lot of moisture. This means we have to help Mother Nature out and water our lawns, gardens, trees and shrubs, and, of course, our indoor plants.

Some overall suggestions: Be conservative and don't waste water – we don't have a lot to spare. Amend your soil so it makes more efficient use of the water it is given. (See How–To Tip on page 127.) Mulch your gardens to help them hold moisture. (See How–To Tip on page 115.) As a general rule, clay soil absorbs about ½" of water per hour. Sandy and rocky soil absorbs water much faster, so water more frequently for a shorter duration. Until you understand your particular soil, periodically check moisture levels with your finger. Otherwise, there is a tendency to overwater, which causes oxygen starvation in roots and the plant rots in the soil. The dying plant often looks the same as a plant that is drought–stressed. The best time to water is early in the morning.

Generally, the rule on watering is infrequent, slow, deep watering for all plant material. However, you will need to increase the frequency of watering during hot periods and reduce the frequency during winter dormant months.

HOW-TO TIPS

Plant	How To Water
Lawn	Kentucky bluegrass needs 24" to 30" of water per year. As a general rule, water 1+" per week during the 20 or so prime growing weeks of the year (mid–spring to mid–fall). The length of time you water is simply long enough for the lawn to collect 1" of water. Of course, watch local weather patterns; decrease water amounts during rainy periods and increase during drought periods. To test how much water your lawn is getting, set out plastic containers in several areas, turn on the sprinkler or sprinkler system, and see how long it takes for 1" of water to collect in the container. Periodically, also test by inserting a screwdriver into the ground in several locations. If the soil isn't damp 6" to 8" down, increase the water, and if it's too wet, decrease the water. Lawns need water when footprints show on the lawn and/or the lawn turns a darker purple–blue color. Do not start watering too early because it could lead to an increase in diseases.
Perennial Flowers, Annual Flowers, Bulbs	Start by clustering plants together that have similar watering requirements in beds. (Look at the label on the plant when you buy it.) The best way to water in the summer is with a drip–emitter system, or with a soaker hose at the base of the plants. Transplants can be watered frequently, lightly. Larger, more developed plants need to be soaked thoroughly, which means the soil should be damp at least 4" to 6" deep. To test, periodically dig down 6" in various parts of your garden to see whether the soil is damp. If it's too dry, increase the water; if it's too wet, decrease the water. In both cases, make sure the soil has been properly amended. In the winter, on a warm day (above 50°), water beds that don't have snow on them. Do this about once a month.
Trees, Shrubs	If trees and shrubs are planted in the lawn, chances are they are getting enough water. Test as you would for the lawn. Thoroughly water new or transplanted trees and shrubs when first planted so the soil will settle. Newly planted trees may need watering once every third day in hot summer temperatures, depending on the type of soil. Then water every seven to ten days during late spring through early fall the first year. Water with drip–emitters or the hose. Deep water during the winter months (see page 113) for the first two winters if the ground is not frozen. After the first 1½ to 2 years, trees should be well–enough established so that no additional watering is needed. Some shrubs may need additional watering, so check them all periodically.

HOW-TO TIPS

Plant	How To Water
Roses	Water a minimum of 1" per week during the growing season. Water heavily every three days, rather than lightly every day. Thoroughly water new or transplanted roses when first planted so the soil will settle. The best way to water is with a drip–emitter system, or with a soaker hose at the base of the roses. To test, periodically dig down 4" to 6" in your rose beds to see whether the soil is damp. Water in the winter as needed.
Drought–Tolerant Gardens	If you use native plant materials or buffalograss in your landscape, you can halve the amounts of water listed above. Watering for the first two years, while plants are getting established, still is recommended.
Kitchen Gardens	After planting seeds, water daily with a hand–held hose or water wand. After seedlings appear, water every day in sandy soil and every other day in loamy or clay soil. Water enough to keep the soil damp about 6" to 8" deep. During hot summer months, water gardens daily. Test by digging down 8" in your garden to see whether the soil is damp. Vegetables that receive irregular or limited watering can be bitter tasting. Tomatoes are particularly sensitive and may develop blossom–end rot if growth occurs under irregular watering conditions.
Interior Plants	Most foliage and flowering houseplants should be watered once a week, and the soil kept evenly moist. However, there are exceptions such as cacti, succulents, bromeliads, etc. (Consult with your garden center or nursery.) Do not let the soil dry out between waterings. To start off, water your plant and come back in four hours. If there is no water in the saucer, water again. In high–light environments, there should be enough standing water in the saucer that the plant can gradually use it for the next two to three days. (The saucer will then be empty.) In low light, there should be enough standing water in the saucer that the plant uses it in one day. Do not mist your plants – it creates false expectations.

HOW-TO TIPS

How To Amend New Mexico Soil

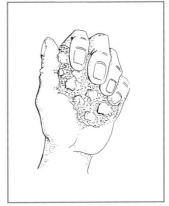

New Mexico soil is not as garden–friendly as soil in other states. To begin with, our soils have a high pH. This is a problem because nutrients needed for growth are bound up in the soil. In addition, New Mexico soil is either too compact (clay), or not compact enough (rocky or sandy). Clay soils have a tendency to compact, driving out needed oxygen to roots. They also hold water. Sandy soils, on the other hand, do not hold water and leach valuable nutrients from the soil. The result, in either case, is that many gardening plants may not be healthy. (There are exceptions to this, especially with native "drought–tolerant" plants.)

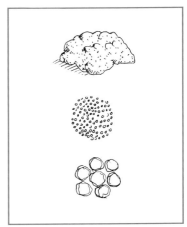

So the soil must be amended. In all cases, the amending is the same, but goals are different. With clay, the goal is to add materials that will loosen up or get air into the soil and lower the pH. With sandy or rocky soil, the goal is to add materials that will cause the soil to retain water and nutrients. The first question is what type of soil do you have in your landscape? Grab a small handful of damp soil and squeeze it. If the soil feels a little sticky and forms a ball, you have clay soil. If it breaks apart into small pieces and feels rather gritty, you have sandy soil. If the soil contains pieces of rock or small rocks, you have rocky soil.

Ｈｏｗ-ｔｏ ＴＩＰＳ

To improve New Mexico soil, add organic soil amendments like compost (see How–To Tip on page 111), or dairy or barnyard manure that is at least one year old. (Never use stockyard manure because it contains too much salt, and mountain peat is too fine to use as a soil amendment.) The general rule is to add one–third organic material to two–thirds existing soil, or three cubic yards per 1,000 square feet each year. (This is about 1¼" of material on top of the ground.) You must till the organic material into the soil, at least 6" to 8" deep, and up to 12" for really healthy soil. Till when the soil is damp, not wet or dry. If it sticks to the shovel, the soil is too wet. (It's difficult to use a tiller in mountain soil because rocks can break the tines. Instead use either heavy equipment or hand dig your soil.)

New Mexico also has a soil phenomenon known as caliche. Caliche is a calcium carbonate (whitish) hardpan ranging in thickness from 1" to several inches. It is found underneath the surface of the soil. If you have caliche running through your soil, serious problems may occur: It will tie up the nutrients, cause poor drainage, and/or the roots of the plant won't establish themselves. You can sometimes break up caliche by tilling it; if not, punch holes throughout your garden and add plenty of organic compost.

HOW-TO TIPS

New Mexico Insects and Diseases

Insect or Disease	How To Identify	What To Do
Aphids	Tiny pear–shaped insects; grow in clusters on leaves; emit sticky substance; cause yellowed, withered, or curled leaves.	Spray hard with water every few days for two weeks for outdoor plants. Use insecticidal soap. Alcohol wash for indoor plants: Use 70% rubbing alcohol straight (no water), spray on infected plant leaves, (test one leaf on each plant first for three days), wait ten minutes, then wash off the aphids with water. (The alcohol forces them to "let go," so it's important to then wash them off completely with water.)
Fungus Gnats	Tiny little gnats that fly around; usually attack interior plants.	Remove all debris from the plant — dead leaves, etc. Make sure plant isn't overwatered. Insect strips (yellow sticky paper): they are attracted to the color yellow.
Lawn Insects and Diseases		See Lawn Maintenance Calendar. Bacillus thuringiensis (Bt)* will work for many lawn insects. Check with lawn care experts or county extension office for correct identification and current recommendations for both insects and diseases.
Mealy Bugs	Bugs that look like little white cotton beads clustered in groups.	Use insecticidal soap. Soap wash (see Spider Mites). Insect strips. Use a cotton tip dipped in alcohol and touch each mealy bug for indoor plants (see Aphids).

How-to Tips

Insect or Disease	How To Identify	What To Do
Pine Tip Moth	The candles on pine trees stop growing and die. First appears in mid–spring and about every six weeks after that.	Spray with a systemic, or Bt. The county extension office will notify local papers and garden centers when they first appear.
Pinon Needle Scale	Black dots on the needles of the pinon tree.	In early spring, a large grayish mass of crawler scale will slowly move up the trunk. As the mass starts to move up the trunk, spray or apply dormant oil with a brush.
Powdery Mildew Black Spot	A fungus that covers leaves and stems with a white powder. Roses are particularly susceptible. A fungus that causes black spots to appear on the leaves of roses.	Light horticultural oil (read label carefully). Baking soda wash: 1 tablespoon baking soda mixed with 1 gallon of water. Spray on infected plants. You also can mix 2 ½ tablespoons of light horticultural oil with 1 tablespoon of baking soda and add to 1 gallon of water. (Test one leaf on each plant first for three days.) If these remedies don't work, try a commercial fungicide.
Scale	Small, brown bumps with hard covering. They emit a sticky substance.	Use insecticidal soap (only works during crawler stage). Scrape off scale with kitchen scrubbie. Alcohol wash for indoor plants (see Aphids). Dormant oil spray. If nothing works, consult with a professional.

HOW-TO TIPS

Insect or Disease	How To Identify	What To Do
Spider Mites	Leaves are mottled with a speckled appearance on the underside of leaves.	Sign of drought stress – check water levels. Use insecticidal soap. Soap wash: mix 1 ounce mild dishwashing detergent (like Ivory) with 23 ounces of warm water, mix well and spray on plant, wait ten minutes, then wash off. Repeat procedure once a week for three weeks. Alcohol wash for indoor plants (see Aphids). Or, simply blast cold water with the hose on the infested plants in the heat of the day.
Tree Diseases	There are over fifty diagnosed diseases and insects that attack trees and shrubs in New Mexico.	If preventative measures fail (suitable species for location, properly amended soil, proper watering and maintenance), call tree experts, or your county extension service for a correct diagnosis and solution.
Whiteflies	Tiny white insects that can be seen in groups under new leaves of a plant. They like the color yellow.	Use insecticidal soap. Insect strips. Alcohol wash for indoor plants (see Aphids). Nasturtiums (they are a trap crop for whiteflies).

*Bacillus thuringiensis (Bt) is an organic microbial insecticide that kills numerous garden insects. It is nontoxic to mammals and for the most part, won't harm beneficial insects (don't use it near butterfly caterpillars!). There are various strains of Bt that are pest specific. Read the label for what pests each strain will attack, or ask your nursery or garden center which should be used.

NOTES

LISTS AND CALENDARS

CHECKLIST

TREES AND SHRUBS IN NEW MEXICO

1. What is your budget? Trees and shrubs can be very expensive, so it's important to know up-front how much money you can afford to spend.

2. Where in the landscape will the tree be planted? What is the microclimate where you live, and what tree will fit best in the location you have chosen? Will the tree grow well in your microclimate?

3. What is your lifestyle? What's going to happen in your landscape? Is it just for show? Do you have kids? A dog? What activities take place outside your home — entertainment, sports, gardening?

4. What colors do you like? Plan for color during all four seasons. What textures do you like? Plan for textures during all four seasons.

5. What are your personal likes and dislikes? Do you like fruit? Do you eat berries? Do you make preserves or cook with items from the garden? Do you like dried arrangements?

6. What are your perceptions of water and watering? Will you take the time to water correctly and properly?

7. Maintenance: How much time will you spend caring for your trees and shrubs? Do you have local water restrictions?

8. What is your time-frame from planting to maturity, i.e., how long will you live in your home?

Trees and Shrubs in New Mexico

Trees and shrubs represent the versatility in any landscape. They can be what you want them to be: they are soft, they are strong, they define, they provide diversion. No matter what kind of setting you want to create, trees and shrubs are important for a landscape that is pleasing to the eye.

Benefits: Part of the role that trees and shrubs play in the environment is to reduce pollution. They also add oxygen to the air, as do all plants, through photosynthesis. Trees are coolants, shading other plants, wildlife, and people.

No other plants can provide the New Mexico landscape with as much depth and variety of color and texture for four seasons.

Type/Structure: Expectations are the most important consideration when planting trees and shrubs. Because they are more of an investment than other types of plants, identifying your own needs and desires before purchasing is highly important. It's difficult to just move a tree after a few years because there was no thought given in the beginning about where it was planted.

Location is Key: It dictates the kind of soil in an area, the exposure (how much sun, what times of the day), the amount of water the plant gets, and diseases. It's also important to note what will be near the tree, and what will eventually be growing under the tree. After you've decided where you want to plant a tree or shrub, take some additional time to shop for the best plant for that location. It is very difficult to successfully transplant trees and shrubs in New Mexico.

Shopping for Trees and Shrubs: Some things to look for:
- Is the soil around the root ball damp (not soaking wet or dry)?
- Are the trees and shrubs all standing upright (not tipped over or lying on their sides)?
- Is the place you are buying from well-maintained?
- Is there any browning on deciduous or evergreen trees?
- Do you know what a fully-grown specimen of what you're buying looks like?
- Is the tree suitable for the growing zone you live in?
- Is a warranty offered on the tree or shrub?
- Is the plant well-rooted?
- Is it hardened-off for your present weather conditions?
- Are there any signs of pests on the tree or shrub?

Insects and Diseases: There are many insects and diseases that can affect trees and shrubs. Some are more life-threatening than others. The key is to continually inspect your trees and shrubs to make sure you catch problems early and then treat them as necessary. A targeted approach is best, taking into consideration the plant species and the insect or disease. If in doubt, ask your garden center or a tree specialist for help!

TREES AND SHRUBS IN NEW MEXICO
Best

EVERGREEN TREES AND SHRUBS	WATER NEEDS
20'+ TALL	
Pinon	Low
Rocky Mountain juniper	Low
Austrian pine	Low/moderate
Southwest white pine	Low
Blue spruce	Moderate
Bald cypress (lower elevations)	Moderate
5' TO 20'	
Curlleaf mountain mahogany	Low
Yews	Moderate
Pyracantha	Moderate
Spanish broom	Low/moderate
Photinia (lower elevations)	Moderate
Nandina (lower elevations)	Moderate/high
UNDER 5'	
Oregon grape	Moderate
Mugo pine	Low
William Penn barberry	Moderate
Barberry (lower elevations)	Moderate
Gray leaf cotoneaster (lower elevations)	Low/moderate
Yucca baccata	Low

DECIDUOUS TREES	
30'+ TALL	
Western catalpa	Low
Western hackberry	Low/moderate
Ash (green and white varieties)	Moderate
English oak	Moderate
Autumn blaze maple	Moderate
London plane tree (lower elevations)	Moderate/high
Shumandi oak (lower elevations)	Moderate
Honey locust	Moderate
Japanese pagoda tree	Moderate

DECIDUOUS TREES	WATER NEEDS
UP TO 30'	
Hawthorns	Low/moderate
Goldenrain	Low/moderate
Flowering crabapple varieties	Moderate
Western River birch	Moderate
Desert willow (lower elevations)	Low
Purple robe locust	Low
Purple leaf plum	Moderate

DECIDUOUS SHRUBS	
10'+	
Gamble oak	Low
New Mexico olive	Low
Amur chokecherry	Moderate
Serviceberry	Low/moderate
Viburnums	Moderate
Chaste tree (lower elevations)	Low/moderate
Yellow bird of paradise (lower elevations)	Low

4' TO 10'	
Fernbush	Low
Chamisa	Low
Apache plume	Low
Cotoneaster	Moderate
Rocky Mountain sumac	Low
Purple leaf sandcherry	Moderate
Western sandcherry	Moderate

UP TO 4'	
Chokeberry	Moderate
Leadplant	Low
Blue mist spirea	Low/moderate
Gro low sumac	Low/moderate
Russian sage	Low

XERISCAPE GARDEN
Best and Worst List

TREES

BEST

Purple robe locust
Pinon pine
Golden rain tree
Austrian pine
Catalpa

Hackberry
Bristlecone pine
Hawthorn
Serviceberry

WORST

Aspen
Cottonwood
Birch
Beech
Magnolia
Willow

SHRUBS

BEST

Mountain mahogany
Buffaloberry
Cliffrose
Blue mist spirea
Lilac
Rabbitbrush
Brooms
Sagebrush
Sumac

Yucca
Apache plume
Currant
Fernbush
Leadplant
Peashrub
Shrub roses
Saltbrush
Butterfly bush

WORST

Deutzia
Hydrangea
Mockorange
Hybrid roses
Spirea
St. John's wort
Weigela
Rhododendron
Tamarisk

FLOWERS

BEST

Penstemon
Hardy iceplant
Aster
Purple coneflower
Pussytoes
Rockcress
Snow-in-summer
Dianthus
Desert zinnia
Gaillardia
Sun rose
Coral bells
Lavender
Blue flax
Poppy mallow

Yellow columbine
Sedum
Daisy
Sage
Jupiter's beard
Coreopsis
Fleabane
Daylily
Bearded iris
Torch lily
Paperflower
Four o'clocks

WORST

Monkshood
Snow-on-the-mountain
Japanese anemone
Astilbe
Hosta
Goatsbeard
Bergenia
Hardy ferns
Black snakeroot
Bleeding heart
Meadowsweet
Euonymous
Siberian iris
Ligularia
Japanese spurge
Creeping buttercup

MOUNTAIN GARDEN
Best and Worst List

BEST

Ponderosa pine
Douglas fir
Pinon pine (some areas)
Limber pine
Lodgepole pine
Bristlecone pine
Narrowleaf cottonwood
Aspen
Norway maple
Amur maple
Rocky Mountain maple
Crabapple
Apple
American plum
Locust
Black locust
Thimbleberry
Peking cotoneaster
Three leaf sumac
Shrub roses
Rugosa roses
Moonshine yarrow
Bluejay columbine
Prof. Kippenberg fall aster
Karl Foerster feather reed
    grass
Moonbeam coreopsis
    (threadleaf)
Leopard's bane
Showy evening primrose
Giant flowered penstemon
May Night salvia
Blue butterfly pincushion
    flower

Peter Davis juniper thyme
Woolly Veronica
Snowdrops
Windflower anemone
Dove columbine
Japanese painted fern
White Clips carpathian
    bellflower
Hardy yellow iceplant
Blue fescue grass
Firecracker penstemon
Silver sage
Rock soapwort
Autumn Joy sedum
Clematis
Bowels periwinkle

WORST/MARGINAL

Broadleaf evergreens
Colchicum (marginal)
Hibiscus
Buddleia
Apricot trees
Upright juniper (deer
    food)
Pyracantha
Forsythia (bloom too
    early)
Rose tree of China
Hybrid tea roses
St. John's wort
Buffalograss
Ceratostigma
Pachysandra
Zinnia grandiflora
Autumn fern
Carex grasses
Ilex
Sweetgum tree
Linden tree
Tree lilac
Catalpa
Marigolds (marginal)
Boston ivy

PATIO GARDEN
Best and Worst List

TREES: Considerations include size, shading characteristics, accenting/enclosure, and leaf/berry drop.

BEST

Honey locust
Golden rain tree
Spring snow crabapple
Montmorency cherry
Thornless cockspur hawthorne

Japanese tree lilac
Ginnala maple
Serviceberry
Foxtail pine
Character pines, dwarf conifers

WORST

Russian olive
Willows
Blue spruce
Fruit trees that drop messy fruit

SHRUBS: Considerations include size, leaf and winter stem texture, flower and leaf color, fragrance, and seasonal interest. Most of the larger shrubs are not suggested unless used as an accent planting.

BEST

Dwarf Korean lilac
Cistena plum
Burkwood viburnum
Roses
Anthony Waterer spirea

Dwarf burning bush
Kelsi dogwood
Russian sage
Low growing junipers
Dwarf barberry

WORST

Alder
Beautybush
Common ninebark
Pfitzer juniper
Pyracantha

PERENNIALS AND GROUND COVERS: These provide the most diversity of plants to consider around the patio garden and are a matter of personal preference. The worst plants are listed primarily because they can be too big, too aggressive, or their texture and size might not fit a patio garden.

BEST SUN

Lavender
Salvia
Coreopsis
Dianthus deltoides
Dwarf asters

Campanula carpatica
Dwarf ornamental grasses
Alpine and Icelandic poppies
Columbine

WORST SUN

Bee balm
Delphinium
Large ornamental grass
Oriental poppy
Yarrow

BEST SHADE

Astilbe
Coral bells
Euonymus coloratus
Mahonia repens
Vinca/Periwinkle

Dwarf bleeding heart
Ferns
Hosta
Lamium
Sweet woodruff

WORST SHADE

Anemone (buttercup)*
Moneywort*
Potentilla verna*
Aegopodium (Bishops Weed)*

*These ground covers are all aggressive and will crowd out a mixed perennial garden. They can be used as a mass planting under shrubs/trees.

INTERIOR GARDEN
Best and Worst List

BEST

SOUTH WINDOWS
Cactus
Lemon tree
Orange tree
Copperleaf
Fiddle leaf fig
Rubber plant
Geranium
Pony tail palm
Strawberry geranium
Dracaenas (many species)
Succulents (aloe, jade,
   donkey's tail)

EAST WINDOWS
Dieffenbachia
Fiddle leaf fig
Nephthytis
Strawberry begonia
Dracaenas (many species)
Moth orchids
Philodendron

WEST WINDOWS
Fiddle leaf fig
Succulents
Dracaenas (many species)
Ficus trees
Philodendron

NORTH WINDOWS
Cast iron plant
Chinese evergreen (Aglaonema)
Mother-in-law's tongue
Bamboo palm
Parlor palm
Kentia palm
Dracaenas (many species)
Philodendron

WORST
Baby tears
Pineapple bromeliad
Starlite bromeliad
Birdsnest fern
Boston fern
Fluffy ruffles fern
Heather
Calathea (prayer plant family)

WINTER GARDEN
Best and Worst List

BEST

Apache plume (white bark)
Oregon grape
Shrub roses (rose hips)
Red twig dogwood (red bark)
Cranberry cotoneaster (red berries)
Specialty conifers
Blue avena grass
Maidengrass
Hardy pampas grass
Heavy metal switchgrass
Karl Foerster reed grass
Blue chip juniper
Broom (moonlight)
Blue mist spirea

WORST

Potentilla
Holly (Ilex)
Rhododendron
Ribbon grass
Arnold's Red honeysuckle

ROSE GARDEN
Best and Worst List

BEST

A Few Hybrid Teas
- Black Garnett
- Lemon Spice (fragrant)
- Mister Lincoln
- Timeless (fragrant)
- Oklahoma
- Pascali
- Pristine
- Yankee Doodle

A Few Floribundas
- Europeana
- Ivory Fashion
- Sunfire
- Gene Boerner
- Redgold
- Sunsprite

A Few Grandifloras
- Camelot
- Prima Donna
- Gold Medal

A Few Miniatures
- Baby Ophelia
- Cupcake
- Green Ice
- Single's Better
- Magic Carrousel
- Mary Marshal
- Rainbow's End
- Valerie Jean

A Few Climbers
- Altissimo
- Blaze
- New Dawn
- Zephirine Drouhin
- America
- Golden Showers
- White Dawn

A Few Miniature Climbers
- Jeanne Lajoie
- Ruby Pendant

A Few Old Garden Shrub and Species Roses
- Applejack (Shrub) (huge)
- Celestial (Alba) (once-blooming)
- Crested Jewel (Moss) (one long blooming)
- Dortmund (Kordesii)
- Fruhlingsmorgen (Hybrid Spinosissima)
- Gertrude Jekyll (English)
- Graham Thomas (English)
- Henry Hudson (Hybrid Rugosa)
- Lilian Austin (Shrub)
- Mme. Hardy (Damask)
- Morden Blush (Alba)
- Rosa Eglanteria (Species)
- Rosa Rugosa Rubra (or Alba Rugosa)
- Sydonie (Hybrid Perpetual)
- Blush Damask (Damask)
- Golden Wings (Shrub)
- Hansa
- Jens Munk (Hybrid Rugosa)
- Linda Campbell (Hybrid Rugosa)
- Paul Neyron (Hybrid Perpetual)
- Morden Centennial (Shrub)
- Rosa Glauca (Species)
- Sally Holmes (Shrub)
- William Baffin (Kordesii) (huge)

WORST

Hybrid Teas
- Blue Girl
- Medallion
- Sterling Silver

Miniatures
- Black Jade
- Judy Fischer
- Rose Window

Climbers
- Dorothy Perkins (mildew-prone)
- Paul's Scarlet

Old Garden
- Souv. de la Malmaison (winter tender)
- Suzanne (spreads uncontrollably)

GREAT ORNAMENTAL GRASSES, BULBS, AND ROCK GARDEN PLANTS

GREAT ORNAMENTAL GRASSES
Feather reed grass
Overdam reed grass
Blue fescue

Blue avena grass
Hardy pampas grass
Japanese blood grass

Maiden grass
Little bluestem grass
Mexican feather grass

GREAT BULBS
Autumn crocus
Bearded iris
Allium
Cannas

Species tulip
Siberian iris
Daffodils
Dahlias

Gregeii tulip
Crocosmia
Hyacinths

GREAT ROCK GARDEN PLANTS

ANNUALS
Dianthus
Summer flowering vinca

Moss rose

Alyssum

PERENNIALS
Penstemon
Phlox

Cranesbill geranium
Sedum

Snow-in-summer
Perennial verbena

BULBS
Species tulips
Muscari hyacinths

Crocus

Daffodils

ORNAMENTAL GRASS
Blue avena

Feather reed grass

Overdam reed grass

TREES AND SHRUBS
Specialty evergreens
Shrub roses

Spreading cotoneasters

Coralberries

GROUND COVERS
Germander

Sedum

Hardy iceplant

GREAT GROUND COVERS FOR NEW MEXICO

PLANT	WATER NEEDS
Sedums	Low
Hen and chicks	Low
Snow-in-summer	Moderate
Ajuga	Moderate
Desert zinnia	Low
Gray and green santolina	Low
Germander	Moderate
Fringed sage	Low
Prairie sage	Low
Powis castle	Low
Hardy iceplants	Low
Catnip	Low/moderate
Wooly and creeping thyme	Moderate
Creeping rosemary	Moderate
Green yarrow	Low/moderate
Pussytoes	Moderate
Kinnickinic	Moderate
Creeping phlox	Moderate
Turkish and wooly Veronicas	Moderate
Saponaria	Moderate
Creeping mahonia	Moderate
Sulfer flower	Low
Vinca minor and major	Moderate
English ivy	Moderate
Low cotoneasters	Moderate
Low junipers	Low/moderate
Mat penstemon	Low

CHILES YOU CAN GROW IN NEW MEXICO

CHILE	AVERAGE SIZE	AVERAGE HEAT
Nu Mex R. Naky	6"	Mild
Big Jim	12"	Mild / medium
Chimayo	6"	Medium
Espanola Improved	5"	Medium
New Mexico 64	7"	Medium
Sandia	6"	Medium / hot
Jalapeno	3" to 4"	Medium hot / hot
De Arbol	2" to 4"	Hot
Mirasol	3" to 4"	Hot
Serrano	2" to 4"	Hot
Habanero	1" to 3"	Very, very hot
Ancho	4" to 5"	Good for rellenos

WHAT BLOOMS WHEN? CALENDAR

SPRING
Alyssum "Basket of Gold" (early)
Creeping phlox (early)
Angelita daisy (late)
Asters (depending on variety) (late)
Blue flax (late)
Blackfoot daisy (late)
Blanket flower (late)
Coreopsis (late)
Evening primrose (depending on variety) (late)
Penstemons (depending on variety) (late)
Paperflower (late)
Oriental poppy
Shasta daisy (late)
Valerian (late)
Veronica (depending on variety) (late)

SUMMER
Aster (depending on variety)
Black-eyed Susan
Blackfoot daisy
Blanket flower
Coneflower
Coreopsis
Coral bells
Chrysanthemum (late)
Desert zinnia
Daylilies
Evening primrose (depending on variety)

SUMMER
Four o'clocks
Iris (early)
Lambs ear
Lavender
Poppy mallow
Plumbago
Penstemons (depending on variety)
Paperflower
Red-hot poker
Shasta daisy
Valerian
Veronica (depending on variety)
Yarrows
Whirling butterflies

FALL
Angelita daisy
Aster (depending on variety)
Blackfoot daisy
Blanket flower
Coreopsis
Coral bells
Chrysanthemum
Desert zinnia
Evening primrose (depending on variety)
Four o'clocks
Poppy mallow
Paperflower

LAWN MAINTENANCE CALENDAR

January	Infrequent, deep watering.
February	Slowly increase watering. Albuquerque and south use pre-emergent* fertilizer, de-thatch and aerate.
March	Water as needed. Santa Fe and north use pre-emergent* fertilizer, de-thatch, and aerate.
April	Increase watering. Watch for weeds.
May	Water regularly and deeply. Albuquerque and south, second feeding of pre-emergent* fertilizer. Warm season grass feeding.
June	Check for dry spots. Santa Fe and north, second feeding of pre-emergent* fertilizer.
July	Water regularly and deeply. Check for dry spots. Start looking for grub activity.
August	Regular watering. All areas, third feeding of pre-emergent* fertilizer. Look for grub activity.
September	Regular watering. Warm season grasses second feeding.
October	Water as needed. Santa Fe and north, feed with a winterizer fertilizer.
November	Infrequent deep watering. Albuquerque and south, feed with a winterizer fertilizer.
December	Infrequent, deep watering.

Lawn diseases to watch for: Dollar spot, brown spot, leaf spot, melting out, and more.

How to identify lawn diseases: Take a sample and description to your local garden center or call your county extension agent.

Preventative measures against lawn diseases: Don't water in the evenings; don't over or under fertilize; de-thatch your lawn; once you note a problem with your lawn, take care of it immediately before the disease or fungus spreads.

Lawn insects to watch for: sod wedworm (spring and summer), white grub (August).

How to identify lawn insects: Unexplained brown spots in lawn, may be due to insects feeding on roots and killing the grass plant.

How to control lawn insects: Chemical treatment is only necessary when the population of insects is high. There are new methods of organic controls. Talk to your local garden center or call your county extension agent.

*Most pre-emergents work by creating a toxic barrier for seeds. If that barrier is established before the seed germinates, the seed will die before it breaks through the soil. That is why it is so important to apply the pre-emergent at the correct time, which is before the seed can germinate.

To prevent crabgrass, apply a pre-emergent before the soil temperature reaches 55° (late winter to early spring). Repeat the application every sixty to ninety days, which is the time period for most pre-emergents to remain active.

Notes

INDEX

ORDER FORM

MONTH–TO–MONTH GARDENING, NEW MEXICO
P.O. Box 3083
Englewood, CO 80155
1-888-GARDEN-8

PLEASE SEND ME: Price   Quantity

MONTH-TO-MONTH GARDENING, NEW MEXICO $22.95   _____
Quantity discounts available when purchasing six or more books.
Call and ask! Wholesale inquiries invited.

SUBTOTAL $ _____
Colorado residents add 3.8% sales tax. $ _____
Add $4.50 for each book for shipping and handling. $ _____

TOTAL ENCLOSED: $ _____

SEND TO

Name _____

Address _____

City _____ State _____ Zip_____

Gift From _____

We accept checks, money orders, Visa or Mastercard (please include expiration date). Please make checks payable to Four Sisters Publishing, Inc. Sorry, no COD orders.

Please charge my ☐ VISA   ☐ MASTERCARD

Card Number _____ Expires_____

Cardholder's Signature _____

CALL TOLL FREE 888–GARDEN–8 FOR INFORMATION ON
MONTH–TO–MONTH GARDENING BOOKS FOR OTHER STATES.